D0804942

MEXICO BY TOUCH

TRUE LIFE EXPERIENCES OF A BLIND AMERICAN DEEJAY

By

Larry P. Johnson

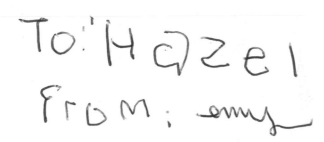
TO: Hazel
From: emmy

© 2003 by Larry P. Johnson. All rights reserved.

No part of this book may be reproduced, stored in a retrieval system, or transmitted by any means, electronic, mechanical, photocopying, recording, or otherwise, without written permission from the author.

ISBN: 1-4107-3591-5 (e-book)
ISBN: 1-4107-3590-7 (Paperback)

This book is printed on acid free paper.

1stBooks – rev. 05/06/03

TABLE OF CONTENTS

INTRODUCTION

My memories of Mexico are a montage of flavors, fragrances, sounds and sensations.

There's nothing that can compare with the smell and taste of freshly made corn tortillas just before the mid-day meal. Nor are there many sounds more soothing and etherial than the rippling melodies of a neighborhood marimba band playing a dawn serenade. But most of all my lasting memories of Mexico are those warm sensations of friendship, fellowship and love given and received.

Stepping off a train in the port of Veracruz, some 45 years ago, I was greeted by a broad-shouldered, barrell-chested, 6 ft. 5 giant who gathered me up in a crushing bear hug, slapped me 4 times affectionately on the backand said, "Welcome!" The man was the cousin of the friend with whom I was traveling, and he wanted me to know straight away that he too was my friend.

At first, I felt a bit self-conscious about being embraced by another man. In my germanic upbringing, I was taught to be more reserved. A polite handshake and verbal salutation was the appropriate greeting. For a man to show his emotions, especially of great joy or deep sorrow, back in the 50's was, in our American culture, considered to be unmanly. But in the Mexican culture, an honest expression of true feelings was believed to be not only natural but desirable. And so, I learned the Mexican "abrazo" or bear hug. Soon it became second nature to me.

My wife and I taught the custom to our children. And now, not a one of them wil enter or leave our presence without giving and receiving a huge hug. It's an expressive way to say "I love you."

"Life is a daring adventure, or it is nothing." (Helen Keller) Before I ever read those words, I believed them and I lived by them.

My adventures in Mexico did not bring me fame or fortune but they did teach me tolerance of small annoyances and inconveniences like earthquakes, power failures, no water or waiting two years to have telephone service.

They also taught me about patience, persistence and appreciation of life's joys and challenges.

I hope my personal journal may inspire, encourage and motivate my readers to follow their dreams and to face life's adversities and challenges with confidence, patience and a sense of humor.

CHAPTER 1 — A MEMORABLE TRAIN RIDE

18, blind, scared and alone in a hotel room in San Luis Potosi, Mexico.

I came awake, paralyzed by fear. Something had touched my face. Something cold and menacing. I lay perfectly still, waiting, listening…

There it was again, something as chilling as death brushing against my cheek. My heart pounded with terror. The muscles around my throat tensed. Drops of sweat rolled off my forehead. A terrifying tingling, numbing sensation spread over my whole body. I did not try to scream. I don't think I could have screamed.

Slowly, struggling against the gripping paralysis of fear, I slid my left hand out from under the covers and bringing it up quickly to my face, I seized the thing of terror. It was a hand! Cold and lifeless!

I laughed out loud. It was mine!

It was July, 1952, and it was my first visit to Mexico.

What made me decide to go? The adventure? That's what I told my family. Yet, in my heart, I knew it was more than that.

Would they have understood, if I could have found the words to describe my desperate yearnings to search for a sense of self-worth, a feeling of personal accomplishment? Did I understand it myself?

Surely I had reasons to be satisfied with my achievements so far. I'd done well in my two years at Wright Jr. College. I had A B-plus average, acted in two school plays and joined a campus fraternity. But, something was lacking. I felt unsatisfied, unfulfilled, wrestless.

I felt I needed to prove something. I needed to prove that I was capable, competent and courageous. I wanted to make my family proud of me. I wanted to show them that, even though I was blind, and the youngest of four siblings, I could do things—things that could cause amazement and admiration.

My Mom taught me, at a very early age, the importance of independence and resiliency. She didn't believe in coddling or shielding me from the bumps and bruises of life just because I happened to be blind.

I remember as a child coming in from play with a bump on my forehead or a cut on my arm and Mom washing off my cuts and bruises, applying the appropriate medication—a piece of ice, a swab of iodine or a Band-Aid—and then sending me right back out to play. It taught me to deal with adversity, to be resilient.

She also taught me that you don't give up easily on something you truly want. And, that year, I had made up my mind that I wanted to go to Mexico.

My two sisters, both older than I, were genuinely concerned about my welfare—about my going off to what they considered to be a strange land of unknown dangers. When I first announced my plan, they tried to persuade our mother to keep me from going. But Mom had faith in me, even more perhaps than I did in myself.

Instead of trying to dissuade me, she sat me down and asked some very direct questions: Where would I stay? What did I plan to do while there? Did I have enough money?

I was ready with my answers. I had it all worked out. I had arranged with the YMCA in Chicago to reserve accommodations for me at the Y in Mexico City. I had written up a budget of daily expenses for the three weeks I would be there. Already in my pocket were my round-trip train ticket and tourist card. And, thanks to a volunteer reader and friend of mine, I had a letter of introduction to a family in Mexico City.

Mom offered a few thoughtful suggestions on what to take along—a supply of canned dog food for Tasha, my guide dog and my portable typewriter so that I could write letters back home.

It was the month before my 19th birthday. Back then, train travel was reliable, comfortable and, for many, the preferred way to go.

The first leg of the journey was a 5-hour trip from Chicago to St. Louis. There, a quick change of trains, and then it was straight on from St. Louis to Mexico City with only a coach change in San Antonio. This through-service, unfortunately, was discontinued sometime in the 1960's.

Although the trip would be a long one, 3 days and two nights, I anticipated no problems for myself. But for Tasha, my 3 year-old Doberman Pincer guide dog, it could be a different story. I had to take along her eating and drinking bowls, cans of dog food and plan when and where we could leave the train so that she could answer to nature's call.

On boarding the train, I talked with the conductor and readily obtained his cooperation. Everything went smoothly while we were on the U.S. side of the border. On crossing over into Mexico, I tried in my limited Spanish to explain to the Mexican conductor our needs to periodically leave the train. He assured me it would be no problem "no problema, senor".

The next morning around 6 a.m., Tasha and I prepared to get off the train as it pulled to a stop in the small town of Bandegas. I asked the conductor if we would have sufficient time for Tasha to enjoy an early morning romp. His reply, as before, was "no problema, senor".

We stepped on to the cindery ground. The air was refreshingly crisp for mid July. Removing Tasha's harness, collar and leash, I lit a cigarette as she scampered off a few yards to relieve herself. Seconds later, I heard two short whistle blasts.

That couldn't possibly be our train, I mumbled to myself. I hesitated, not sure what to do.

Just then, a heavily accented voice spoke to me in English: "Senor, did you want the train?"

Reacting now to the reality of what was happening, I said: "Yes, yes, stop the train."

His reply, soft and musical, stunned me like a blow to the solar plexus. "Oh, senor, the train, she go away."

I stood motionless in disbelief. How could this be happening? I was alone in a foreign country, in a place I didn't know with my baggage on a train to Mexico City. I felt frightened and overwhelmed with doubt. Had I made the wrong decision to travel to Mexico by myself? Had my sisters been right after all? Why hadn't I listened? I could have gone to Des Moines to visit my Aunt Marie, or to California to spend time with Uncle Ted and his family. But no, I chose Mexico.

I told myself it was to improve my knowledge of Spanish. I had studied it my last two years in high school and two more years at Wright Jr. I had made it a habit to listen to Spanish language radio stations in Chicago, and I understood most of what was said. I had joined the Pan American Club, a cultural/social group which met on Saturday afternoon downtown on Michigan Avenue at the Fine Arts building. They offered interesting and entertaining programs in Spanish on the music and customs of Latin America.

But speaking Spanish in the classroom or with acquaintances who are willing to speak slowly and translate words you don't know is one thing. Another is to be totally immersed in an environment where Spanish is the only language.

I wanted adventure. Well, here it was.

The voice spoke again: "I can help you, senor."

"Yes, por favor" (please), I replied. I quickly called Tasha to my side. It felt good to have her with me. As I leaned to fasten the harness under her chest, she lifted her muzzle and licked me on the cheek as if to say, don't worry, I'll get you out of this.

The voice led me to the telegraph office next to the depot, keeping four or five paces ahead of me, out of respect for or fear of Tasha. Dobermans do have a menacing look. If the truth were told however, Tasha was as gentle as a pussycat.

6

Using my limited Spanish and some English I managed to send a message requesting that my baggage be unloaded and held for me in San Luis Potosi, a major city in northern Mexico, about halfway between the U.S. border and the capital, Mexico City.

The next train, I learned, would not be by for 12 hours. What was I to do?

My nameless companion provided the answer. He guided me to a small "posada", a family-owned inn a short distance from the depot. There was a brief exchange between him and the woman owner, so rapidly spoken that I guessed rather than understood what was said. They would take care of the norteamericano and his "perrita" (dog) until the train arrived.

The family consisted of the mother, two teenage daughters and a couple of younger children who squealed nervously at the sight of Tasha. For her part, Tasha exhibited the grace and elegance of a queen, walking with quiet dignity, her head held high. I was so proud of her. I began to feel my own confidence return.

That wonderful family showed me incredible hospitality. They took me into their inn, fed me, brought water to Tasha, gave us a place to rest and when the time came for us to catch our train, they made sure we were at the depot in plenty of time. When I offered them payment, they refused.

7

First impressions are indeed powerful ones. And undoubtedly, because of this wonderful experience of warm Mexican hospitalityand many other similar positive incidents, I returned twice more to Mexico as a tourist and then later to live as a student and resident for 17 years.

CHAPTER 2—TRAIN RIDE 2

Back on the train and again headed for Mexico City, I felt both relief and satisfaction. Tasha and I had survived our first Mexican adventure. I was excitedly, albeit naively, optimistic that we could handle any situation that might come along. I felt confident that Tasha and I were ready for anything.

At around 11 p.m., we pulled into the station at San Luis Potosi. Tasha and I got off the train, headed into the depot to claim my luggage and have it placed back on board.

We were met by two young Mexican men who, while keeping a respectful distance, escorted us to a small baggage room where my two suitcases and portable typewriter were waiting. I gave a quick look at my belongings. "Okay, it's all here. Let's go." I said in Spanish. I was anxious to get back on the train.

"Oh, no, senor. You must check everything carefully," insisted one of the young men.

I responded by dutifully opening each suitcase and probeing the contents with my hands. "It's fine. Everything's here." I repeated, closing the clasps on the second suitcase. "Can we go now please?" I urged.

"No, not yet. You must write a receipt," the second young man instructed.

"A receipt?" I asked.

"Yes, a receipt," explained his companion, "saying that everything has been returned to you in good order."

"But, the train is getting ready to leave," I protested, "and besides, I have nothing to write with."

"The train will wait," they both assured, "and we must have a receipt."

"Okay, okay." I replied with annoyance while snapping open my portable typewriter. "Give me a piece of paper, please."

Paper was produced. I inserted it into the typewriter and began typing in Spanish a short statement to the effect that I had received all of my belongings without omission and in good condition, on this date, in this city, at 11:20 PM. in the presence of these two witnesses. I removed the paper from the typewriter and handed it to the young man nearest me. He read it over carefully and passed it to his companion. Satisfied, they handed it back to me saying: "Very good, now you sign it please."

"Gladly," I agreed. Quickly scribbling my name at the bottom, I returned it to them and got to my feet. "Can we go now?" I asked with impatience.

10

"Of course, of course," they echoed each other. Picking up my suitcases and typewriter, we headed out of the depot and toward the train. But alas! The train was already moving from the platform and gathering speed.

"Not again." I groaned. "Yell for them to stop!" I shouted.

"It's too late, senor. They won't hear us," commented the young man nearest to me. "Not to worry," he reassured me. "We'll take you to a hotel and you can stay there tonight and catch the next train in the morning."

His solution was simple and logical. I now had all my belongings with me, including Tasha's bowls and food. Did it really matter that I would get to Mexico City another half day later than planned? Wasn't this just another part of my adventure?

Tasha and I followed our two guides as they led us from the depot, down a narrow, deserted street for about two blocks and then entered what I assumed to be the lobby of a small, local hotel. One of my escorts approached the desk clerk and spoke with him in low tones for a couple of minutes, most of which I could not hear. I waited.

"The room rate is $3.50 American," he informed me.

I didn't know what kind of place I had been taken to, nor what a reasonable rate for a hotel room in that city was. I was tired and anxious to get some sleep. "Okay, fine." I agreed.

Paying for the room, I received my key and followed the two young men down a long hallway that smelled of insect spray and mildew. "here is your room." They said in unison.

Inserting the key and opening the door, I stepped into a small room containing a bed, bureau, and bathroom. Very plain, very simple. Fine, I thought. What more did I need? Just a place to sleep. That is, if I <u>could</u> sleep.

Although my companions had given me no obvious cause to mistrust them, I felt apprehensive, nonetheless. A wave of paranoia was creeping into my consciousness. I wondered, had this pair deliberately delayed me so that I would miss the train and then be obliged to follow them to this obscure, run-down hotel for some sinister purpose?

"Sleep well, senor. Good night," they said as they turned to leave. There was no offer of we'll see you in the morning and get you to the station on time. Perhaps they were just glad to be rid of me. Or perhaps…they planned to come back later. Oh, my paranoia was getting the better of me.

Closing the door behind them, I removed Tasha's harness and leash. Let someone just try and come through that door uninvited. Tasha would handle them. At least, I hoped she would. She had never been tested in a situation where I was in physical danger. Still, I had faith that her love and loyalty would guide her actions.

12

As an added precaution, I decided to have my trusty Boy Scout knife at the ready, under my pillow, just in case. How naïve. How foolish. What protection would a small penknife be against a couple of strong and determined assailants?

I was 18 and traveling alone only for the second time in my life. The first time had been two years ago when I went to Detroit to receive my beautiful Tasha. That was a lot easier. My Mom took me to the depot. The train ride was just a few hours long, and when I got to Detroit, there was someone from the school to meet me. This time it was different. I was alone in a foreign country with only a limited understanding of the language.

I was determined to put on a brave face. I thought about my hero figures, from radio shows I used to listen to as a kid — Jack Armstrong, Sky King, the Lone Ranger, Captain Midnight. I thought about how they would handle things if they were in my situation. Stay calm and remain alert. That's what they would do. Okay. That's what I'll do.

I fed Tasha and gave her a big bowl of water. Poor thing, she hadn't eaten for nearly two days. Afterward, I laid down to try and get some sleep. During the first hour and a half I tossed and turned, drifting in and out of a restless slumber, mixing images of reality with those from my dreams.

Then, at one point, I came awake, paralyzed by fear. Something had touched my face. Something cold and menacing. I lay perfectly still, waiting, listening...

There it was again, something brushing against my cheek. My heart pounded with terror. The muscles around my throat tensed. Drops of sweat began rolling off my forehead. A terrifying tingling, numbing sensation spread over my whole body. I did not try to scream. I don't know if I could have screamed.

Slowly, with great effort, I slid my left hand out from under the covers. Then, bringing it up quickly to my face, I seized the thing of terror. It was a hand! Cold and lifeless!

It did not resist my grasp. It did not move. Slowly, I followed the connection of the dead hand up to its wrist, there joined to its dead arm and finally up to its right shoulder...which was mine.

On discovering the truth, I laughed out loud. I apparently had slept on top of my arm or it had been dangling off the bed for some time. The result was that lack of blood flow had left the arm without feeling. My mind had magnified and used my own fears, and I was my own intruder.

The next morning, a bellman from the hotel accompanied me back to the depot where I boarded the Aztec Eagle for the third time. Twelve hours later I arrived in Mexico City without further incident.

CHAPTER 3—JUST ANOTHER TOURIST

We pulled into Mexico City in the late afternoon. I took my time gathering my belongings. With Tasha's harness in one hand, I knew I was going to need some help carrying my luggage off the train and finding a taxi to take me to the Y.

As I pondered this problem, I heard my name being called from the end of the car. "Mr. Larry Johnson. Larry Johnson." It was spoken both as a question and as a plaintive pleading. I stood up and acknowledged the call.

"Oh, gracias a Dios" (Thank God.), a young male voice said coming close to me. "My name is Sergio. I am with the YMCA, and I have been sent to meet you. This is the third train I have met."

I thanked Sergio for his persistence and apologized for my delayed arrival. By way of response, Sergio picked up one of my suitcases, my portable typewriter and said "Follow me, please."

He led the way off the train through the depot and to a waiting taxi. As we climbed in, he introduced me to another passenger. "This is my novia (sweetheart). "If you hadn't been on this train either, I had planned to take her to a movie. But, that can wait now."

The Y was located on Valderas Street right in the heart of downtown Mexico City. Sergio got me checked in quickly and then showed me my room. It was on the second floor. A modest accommodation with a chest of drawers, a small desk and chair, a clothes rack, a nightstand and a bed which was too short (as I discovered all beds in Mexico were.). It smelled clean and felt comfortable.

"The showers and rest rooms are down the hall and are shared by all the guests on this floor." He explained. "There's a restaurant on the first floor, which served breakfast, lunch and supper—at moderate prices."

"Where is there a park or a place where I can take Tasha to relieve herself?" I asked.

"There's a lovely park, La Alameda, just across the street from the Y. You can take her there." He said. Having fulfilled his responsibilities to me, and obviously anxious to get back to his novia, he took his leave.

I settled in and got ready to immerse myself in my new environment, to learn about a people and culture which fascinated me, and to be just another typical first-time American tourist.

During my three weeks stay, I met many interesting people and had a rich variety of experiences. There was the Gustavo Rocha family who showed me wonderful hospitality, inviting me to their home one evening for a sumptuous family dinner. On another occasion, on a lovely Sunday afternoon, they took me to enjoy the famous Floating Gardens of Xochimilco, a 40 minute drive from the capital. This area is known as the Venice of Mexico. Floating along in a boat called a "chalupa" similar to the gondolas of Venice, I inhaled the fragrances of food and flowers sold by passing merchants and listened to the music of marimba players and mariachi groups drifting across the water. Years later, when I became a resident of Mexico City, my family and I would repeat this experience many times over. It was, and probably still is, a popular family outing for "capitalinos" residents of the capital.

I had my first drink of tequila one evening at the Y. As I was returning from my dinner with the Rocha family, on the way to my room I met a Mexican fellow who was also staying at the Y. I guessed him to be in his early 50's. He was eager to tell me his views of Mexico's political history. He invited me to his room to share "una copita" a glass of tequila and some conversation. I accepted.

He turned out to be a strong liberal-thinking intellectual. He gave me his perspective of the 1910 Mexican Revolution, the expropriation of foreign oil interests under President Lazaro Cardenas during the 1930's and his assessment of

18

current Mexican politics under the ruling PRI, Institutional Revolutionary Party.

After my third tequila, my stomach began feeling queasy. I thanked my host for his conversation and hospitality and headed quickly for the bathroom, where I promptly lost my dinner. Tequila is awfully potent stuff to the uninitiated.

Tasha and I traveled throughout Mexico City easily and with confidence—on foot, by bus and by taxi. People often would ask me if Tasha would bite "Muerde?" I thought it best to be vague and keep them wondering, and so I would reply "Perhaps".

Asking directions from Sergio or from others at the Y, Tasha and I ventured to the "Mercado de Curiosidades" (Curiosity Market), where I shopped for Mexican onix and silver to take back home.

We visited the "Basilica de Guadalupe" (the famous Shrine and Church of Our Lady of Guadalupe). I was surprised and moved by the large throng of tourists and native-born who came to express their faith and make their petitions to Mexico's patron saint. Some demonstrated their piety and devotion by ascending the rocky slope to the shrine on their knees.

We discovered the "Castillo de Chapultepec" (Chapultepec Castle), once the imperial residence of Maximiliano and Carlota, later a military college for young Mexican army cadets and now a marvelous national museum rich in colonial history. It was there that I met an Austrian-born gay professor from Illinois who befriended me. (I didn't know he was gay at the time.)

He was very knowledgeable about the history of the Aztec and Mayan cultures. Together we visited the National Museum of Anthropology. He was extremely helpful in pointing out important characteristics of the exhibits and in reading the descriptive plaques which accompanied them.

Several months after returning to Chicago I invited him to dinner at our house. Naively, I took him upstairs to our converted attic to show him my record collection of Latin American music. While there, he shocked me by making sexual advances toward me. It was my first encounter with a person overtly homosexual. I rebuffed him and quickly went back downstaris to join my family. I did not tell them what had happened, out of embarrassment, I suppose. That ended our acquaintanceship.

Tasha went with me everywhere in Mexico City except for one, the "Palacio de Bellas Artes" (Palace of Fine Arts). Two other Americans, who were also staying at the Y, invited me to join them for a concert at the Palace of Fine Arts. I agreed. Arriving at the entrance, we were told that "dogs were not allowed".

I explained that Tasha was no ordinary dog, that she was my guide dog, my eyes. The employee stood his ground and refused us admittance. My companions urged me to attend the concert without Tasha. Reluctantly, I took a taxi back to the Y where I left Tasha by herself and returned to hear the concert. I had tremendous pangs of guilt over this and vowed not to abandon her again.

And, of course, I will always remember Lupita, a beautiful young girl, also just 18. She was a waitress in the restaurant at the Y. My heart was easily won over by her attentive and flirtacious manner. She would take my hand and gently place it on the silverware or glass or cup which she brought me and tell me its name in Spanish. Her voice was soft, like a sweet caress. I was ready to be in love, but I felt frustrated by my limited vocabulary in Spanish and my basic shyness toward girls.

I told her nothing, but back in my room sitting at the small desk, I wrote the lyrics to a love song in Spanish, "El Dolor de Amor" (The Pain of Love), which she never heard.

There would be two more visits to Mexico as a tourist before I became a legal, full-time student and resident in 1957. It would be then that my career as the first blind American deejay in Mexico City would commence.

CHAPTER 4 — A SAILOR TO THE RESCUE

Studying Spanish in high school came very easily for me. But it almost also became my downfall.

It was 1946. I'd just turned 13 and was beginning my freshman year at John Marshall High School on Adams Street, on Chicago's near westside. My teachers persuaded my mother that Latin was a good base for developing mental agility, for learning any future languages and for doing well in mathematics. So, I was signed up to take Latin my freshman year. I had no say in the matter.

It wasn't too bad that first year. In fact, I did quite well. But by the second year, I began losing interest. And, as my interest declined, so did my grades.

I also began to doubt that Latin was as important as my teachers had said. Except for the Catholic Church and the Latin club, there weren't any places where you could find Latin being spoken.

Toward the end of the second semester of my sophomore year, my Latin teacher, clearly aware of my declining interest and grades, asked if I planned to take Latin my junior year. I told her no. I'm sure she felt this was a wise decision and rewarded me by giving me a final grade just above failing.

I was grateful of course, but my ego had been injured. I felt I needed to prove to myself, and to others as well, that I wasn't totally stupid when it came to learning languages.

Several of my friends were studying Spanish and seemed to really enjoy it. They weren't struggling with it the way I had been struggling with Latin. Spanish appeared to be more useful and more fun. People actually spoke it around town. Chicago had then, and still does have, a large Spanish-speaking community. So, I decided to take Spanish my junior year.

That first year went very, very well indeed. I earned excellent grades. In retrospect, I have to admit that studying Latin first probably had a lot to do with the ease with which I picked up Spanish, although I wouldn't have admitted it at the time.

My senior year was a year of play, of disregard for rules, and of challenges—challenges to authority. Seniors think they know it all and believe they are invincible. It was toward the end of my fourth semester in Spanish that my teacher, Ms. Sailor, caught me cheating on a test.

The usual procedure for us blind students to take a test was to pick it up from the classroom teacher and go down to our resource room where we would do it on our own, on the honor system. Having a textbook in braille there in the resource room was a great temptation, and sometimes, I would sneak a look or two, just to be sure my answer was right, of course. It was easy to do, and it allowed me to finish the test more quickly. Doing tests in this manner though, ill-prepared me to be able to pass a real test later on. That possibility, however, didn't occur to me at the time.

One day, Ms. Sailor decided to give me an oral test. She called me to the back of the room while the rest of the class took the test from the blackboard. She began asking me the questions orally. Not having my braille textbook available, I found it difficult to remember the answers. This aroused her suspicions and eventually brought her to the conclusion that I was not quite as brilliant as my test scores indicated.

"I suspected some funny business was going on with your tests downstairs." She said simply.

My reddening face betrayed my guilt. I was in really hot water, and I knew it. Ms. Sailor had in her hands the power to put a monkey wrench into my plans for graduation. As I sat there exposed to the truth, frightened and ashamed, my heart pounded with agony as I envisioned Ms. Sailor telling my resource teacher, who in turn would call my mother. Eventually the whole class and school would know of my cheating. In my mind I could see the entire senior class marching down the aisle in their caps and gowns, and there I would be sitting in the audience embarrassed and miserable.

I'd have to return for another semester to the same school and face my disgrace.

Ms. Sailor must have seen the fear and remorse on my face. In any event, she chose not to report me. Or if she did, it was never made public. She did not stand in the way of my receiving my high school diploma, and for that, I am eternally grateful to her.

The day before graduation, I went to her classroom. I found her alone. I thanked her for her compassion and clemency.

Her cryptic response: "I hope you have learned your lesson, Larry."

"Yes ma'am, oh yes ma'am." I replied.

Some five years later, I had the occasion to vindicate her decision and show her my gratitude in a most unusual way. I was riding on a bus in Chicago with a blind musician friend from Mexico, Pompeyo Torres. Pompeyo had come to Chicago with his wife Esther, the daughter of a Swedish Baptist missionary working in Mexico. I met them at a Thanksgiving dinner put on by a local community organization called the Blind Service Association.

Pompeyo knew practically no English. I was very anxious to improve my Spanish, so we struck up an acquaintanceship and agreed to help each other learn the other's language. We spent a lot of time together. In truth, I got the better end of the deal by learning more Spanish from Pompeyo than he learned English from me.

We drank beer together. We rode buses and the "El" together. We spent hours at his place or mine talking about music and people, our different cultures, the history, and future of blind people in his country and mine.

It was while we were riding on a Montrose Avenue bus one afternoon. I was struggling in Spanish to communicate an important point, dealing with I don't now remember what, and I was stuck on finding the right word in Spanish. After a string of "Como se dice? Como se dice? Como se dice?" (How do you say it? How do you say it? How do you say it?) I heard behind me a female voice supplying the precise word in Spanish which I had been searching for. I responded enthusiastically "Yes, that's it. That's the word I wanted," and quickly completed my sentence to Pompeyo. Then I turned to the person behind me and said "thank you."

The female voice said, "You're welcome, Larry. Perhaps you don't remember me. My name is Miss Sailor. I was your Spanish Teacher in high school."

Gulp. I felt a rush of emotions ranging from surprise to embarrassment to appreciation. All I could do in that moment was to stammer "Oh sure. Sure, Miss Sailor, yes I remember you. Thanks, thanks a lot."

As I expressed my appreciation to her for coming to my rescue at that moment with the right word, I hoped that somehow she might also have understood my deeper gratitude for her generous action years earlier. Perhaps because of that second chance, I had been motivated to continue my studies and interest in Spanish. I had taken four more semesters of Spanish in College and was now using it to communicate with someone from another country. If she understood this, she may indeed have smiled a smile of satisfaction, and this episode may have been for her an unexpected and gratifying reward.

CHAPTER 5 — A SIDE ADVENTURE OR... THERE WILL ALWAYS BE A PART OF ME IN OLD MEXICO

My second trip to Mexico occurred in 1955. Again I traveled by train, but this time it was in the company of a young lady.

Her name was Elsa. She was a friend of Pompeyo and Esther's and attended the same church that they did. (My beloved Tasha had departed from my side six months earlier due to an illness.)

Esther and Pompeyo proposed the idea of Elsa and I traveling to Mexico together. The plan was practical and two-fold. First of all, by Elsa acting as my travel guide, we could travel on a special two-for-one travel concession then granted to blind persons through the American Foundation for the Blind and the bus and railway companies. Second, since Elsa knew no Spanish, I could serve as her interpreter once we got across the border. Thus, it was advantageous for us both. We would save money and be of mutual help.

We met about a month and a half before we were to leave on the trip. Elsa lived with her father in a suburban house on the Northwest side of Chicago. She was in her late 20's and unmarried. I was 21. She was of Germanic background and a strong Baptist. Since I was more of a free thinking liberal on matters of religion, I anticipated some rather pithy discussions throughout our trip.

There was a lot of excited conversation as we talked over our plans. Esther and Pompeyo would leave by bus about a month ahead of us so that they could spend more time with their families. Elsa and I would travel by train and be in Mexico for perhaps ten days. That was as much time as she could take off from work, and all that my meager finances would allow.

I was looking forward to this trip for a special reason, to help me forget a recent, heartbreaking romance with a dark-haired, dark-eyed girl from Puerto Rico named Raquel.

Raquel and I had been going together for just over a year. I was deeply in love with her and believed one day we would be married. Then, one evening she told me, without warning, in her quiet sweet voice, we would have to stop seeing each other.

"My parents do not approve", she said. "They do not want me to marry an American boy. I am sorry. I am very fond of you, but I must do what my parents say."

I was devastated, struck dumb. I could think of nothing to say. I knew of instances of prejudice by Americans toward

Puerto Ricans. But, I had never ever imagined it could be the other way around.

I held her tightly, for the last time, and I cried.

Turning from her door, I walked the five miles home in a daze, carelessly crossing streets, oblivious to honking horns and squealing brakes, hoping, praying that my misery and my young life would be ended swiftly and mercifully. My guardian angel was indeed tested that night, and I survived.

About three months later, I called Raquel to ask how she was doing. I was invited to dinner, where I was introduced to her new boyfriend, another American. What she had told me — had been a lie.

I never learned or asked about the real reason for her decision to break off our relationship. Was it my blindness? Was it my not having a car? My not having a full-time job? Perhaps it was all of these, or none of them. It didn't really matter. She had wanted out, and she had lied. The pain was deep, and I needed to forget.

The trip to Mexico with Elsa started off quite uneventfully. I met her at the depot. We purchased our tickets, boarded the train and settled into our first class coach seats. It was the most economical way to travel. The trip, I knew from prior experience, would take two and a half days to the border and then another full day and night from the border to Mexico City. We would be together a long time.

We arrived in St. Louis on time and there boarded the Missouri Pacific which took us as far as Laredo, Texas. There we changed trains again, boarding the Aztec Eagle, the pride of the national railroad of Mexico.

I've always loved trains. There's a freedom you have on a train which you don't have on a bus or airplane. On buses and planes you can't move around very much at all. You have to pretty much stay in your seat. With trains, however, it's different. You can get up and stroll from car to car, meeting interesting people along the way.

I found it was fun and a challenge to walk from one end of the train to the other—through the Pullmans cars, the coaches, the observation car and the dining car—with the train shifting and swaying, trying to keep my balance without having to grab hold of a seat or a table or of somebody's berth. There were perhaps 15 coaches and Pullmans on that train. Each car offered interesting experiences and encounters.

Another favorite thing I loved to do was to stand between the cars with one hand on each door and feel the movement of the couplers beneath my feet as they twisted and turned and bounced along the track. It gave a sensation of the train being alive.

I don't think trains are as much fun as they used to be. Back then, you came across all kinds of travelers—families, servicemen, minor league baseball teams, boy scout troops, retired folks. On this trip I met a rich sampling of all types and really enjoyed our first two and a half days.

Elsa and I spent long hours talking about everything imaginable, including religion, about which we firmly disagreed. I think I enjoyed challenging her fundamentalist views, testing her beliefs, exploring her convictions. Perhaps I was also feeling somewhat cynical and generally resentful toward the opposite sex, considering my crushingly painful, recent experience of rejection by Raquel.

Elsa was a gentle, soft-spoken woman but of very strong will. She had a warm, compassionate nature. She reminded me of a benevolent Sunday school teacher. When I needed her help she was very dependable.

The side effects of my trip to Mexico began making themselves known soon after we crossed the border. I developed a stomachache. At first, I thought that's what it was, a stomachache. I lost my appetite and had trouble sleeping. I spent a lot of time standing and walking about.

The top section of one of the platform doors between the cars was usually open, and I found some relief standing there with the cool breeze blowing against my face. Pressing my side

32

against the cold steel edge of the bottom section of the door also seemed to help. It was the right side of my abdomen, at about belt level.

The thought of appendicitis never entered my mind. I thought it might be a touch of intestinal flu. I longed for us to arrive in Mexico City and to be able to stretch out on a bed and sleep. Elsa was very patient during this time. She didn't know what to make of it either.

On our arrival in Mexico City, we were met at the station by Pompeyo and Esther who helped us collect our luggage and get a cab to the hotel. I told them of my stomach cramps. They offered to arrange for me to see a doctor the next day, if the pain persisted.

That evening, Pompeyo came by with a friend, Raul Garmendia. Raul was also blind. He was a tall, muscular man from the state of Veracruz with a jolly spirit. His big arms and bulging tummy reminded me of a bear. In spite of his evident physical strength, Raul had the gentleness of a lamb and the generosity of a saint. For a friend he would literally give the shirt off his back. He tried his best to cheer me up by telling me numerous off-color Veracruzano jokes. I was not a very good audience.

By the next morning, I had a raging fever and my side was throbbing even more. I was eager to keep the appointment with the doctor that Pompeyo and Esther had arranged for me to see. We went by taxi to his office. Pompeyo told me that in addition to being a full-time physician, Dr. Vallarino had also been director of the National School for the Blind, which is how Pompeyo and Raul came to know him.

Upon arriving at his office, we were ushered into his examining room. I climbed onto the examining table. It was too short. My feet extended about three inches over the edge of the table. This created a lot of laughter. Dr. Vallarino suggested that perhaps his first operation should be to shorten my legs so that I could fit on his table. There was more laughter.

Examining my abdomen, he was quick to diagnose that my condition was acute appendicitis. He told me not to worry, but I was worried. In fact I was downright scared. Here I was in a foreign country and suddenly facing the prospect of an operation. What was I to do?

Dr. Vallarino had already made that decision for me. He would prescribe some penicillin pills to see if this would abate the infection. In a day or two, if all went well, I could fly home and have my appendix out in my own homeland. However, if the medication proved ineffective in controlling the infection, he said, "then you will be one of the privileged few Americans to have the opportunity to experience the skill of the Mexican surgeon's knife".

There was more raucus laughter. It was his way of making light of the situation, so that I would not be overly concerned. My friends Raul and Pompeyo thoroughly enjoyed Dr. Vallarino's carefree prognosis. But I wasn't laughing. I was bewildered. Then, remembering the adventures I experienced on my first trip to Mexico and how I had survived them all, I said to myself Okay, "que sera sera", (whatever will be, will be). Another experience to learn from, another challenge to face.

We headed back to the hotel, stopping at a pharmacy along the way to pick up the penicillin capsules I was to begin taking. I had no appetite and felt nausea when I tried to eat. I supposed it was one of the effects of the appendicitis.

Pompeyo and Raul introduced me to an apple-flavored carbonated soft drink called Sidral which I found to be cool and refreshing. It was about the only nourishment that I could keep down. I was to take the penicillin capsules every four hours as prescribed by Dr. Vallarino. I spent the rest of the day in bed.

Esther and Elsa came by in the evening to offer words of consolation and encouragement. It was becoming increasingly clear though that the penicillin was not doing the job.

By late afternoon the following day, Dr. Vallarino concluded that I would not be able to fly home. The danger of a rupture was too great. He made arrangements for me to be admitted to a small local clinic near his office.

It was Wednesday evening. Pompeyo, Esther and Raul took me to the clinic by taxi. I was in a surprisingly good mental state, quite prepared somehow for this most unusual experience. I felt alert and curious to all that was going on around me. I had not yet advised my family of my situation, knowing how worried my mother would be when she learned that I was to be operated on so far from home, by a strange doctor in a strange land.

The bed in the clinic was again too short for my 6 ft. 4 in. frame. I solved this by laying catty-corner, with my head at the top left corner and my feet at the lower right. Pompeyo, Ester and Raul wished me well and said they would be back to see me in the morning "after the cutting".

My nurse was named Hilda. A relatively short, full-figured girl of about 25, she was from the port of Veracruz like Raul. She had a perpetual smile on her lips and a mischievous twinkle in her voice. She delighted in teasing me in every way that she could during the five days that I was under her care.

The first night she came to my bedside and informed me that she was there to prepare me for the operation the next morning. I did not immediately grasp the meaning of her words. "What do you wish me to do?" I asked.

he answered in a matter of fact manner, "You must take off your shorts, I have to shave you."

"Shave me?" I asked.

"Yes, for the doctor tomorrow."

I gulped once or twice. Was she serious? As she placed a small pan of water on my night stand and sat down on the edge of the bed, I realized that she meant business. I dutifully unclothed from the waist down and modestly turned my head to one side. She began to apply the soap and water and with a straight razor in her right hand began removing all my pubic hair. Good heavens, I thought, how will I control a spontaneous reaction of arousal if her hand should slide across a sensitive area? Then I thought, good heavens, what if her hand holding the razor should slip? The latter thought must have stayed upper most in my mind for I felt no sexual stimulus whatsoever during the ten-minute procedure. We chatted about life in her province and what it was like in the United States. It was the kind of conversation you might have overheard two people having while traveling on a bus or train together.

At one point she had to flip my penis from one side to the other so that she could proceed with the shaving. Because of my lying partially on my side, the penis fell back to its original place. "Disobedient," she scolded.

Embarrassed, I rolled my body toward the other side and allowed gravity to play its role. She finished her job and our conversation ended. What will be next, I thought, in this ever unfolding series of experiences in Mexico?

The next morning she came back, this time to give me an injection. It was a mild sedative which was to get me ready for the operation in about an hour. I felt very relaxed, very confident, very at ease with the whole situation. I wistfully wondered what my mother would say if she could see where I was and what was about to transpire. I had decided to wait and tell her about everything after the fact.

Hilda was back. She asked me to rise from my bed. There was no cart to wheel me to the operating room. I put on my shoes, my robe, and took her arm. We left the room and climbed two flights of stairs to the second florr. I thought to myself, how will they ever get me back down these stairs after the operation? Well, I had trusted everything to fate so far, so I might as well continue doing that.

Outside the operating room I met the anesthetist. He was a young, pleasant fellow who asked me a series of questions about whether I had any history of weak heart, who was my next of kin, etc. — questions that certainly weren't designed to make one feel calm or relaxed. Yet strangely, I felt no alarm or concern. Perhaps the injection I had received from Hilda a few minutes earlier had numbed me to all of this.

Then they were ready for me, and I was ushered into the operating room walking. Dr. Vallarino was waiting there and he greeted me cordially. He took my hand and placed it on the operating table saying: "This is where your head should be. There's where your feet are to be. Now if you would please climb on board."

It all seemed so bizarre. I felt no distress or concern. It was as if it wasn't happening to me—that it was a movie script and I was just one of the actors playing a part.

The anesthetist stuck a needle in my arm and started the flow of sodium pentathol. He asked me to begin counting backwards from 100.

"Shal I count in English or in Spanish?" I asked.

Everyone in the room laughed. The anesthetist said, "No importa". (It doesn't matter.)

So, I began counting in English, starting from 100. The last number I remember was eighty-seven. Then, it was lights out.

My friends told me later that it took four people, one at each end and two in the middle, to carry me back down the two flights of stairs to my guestroom. When I awoke later that day, which was early evening, I had company. I had a roommate, a lady who had just given birth to her first baby. The baby was with her and protesting loudly, either needing to be changed or fed or both. We were separated only by a thin curtain which served very little to muffle the sounds of the howling infant. My head throbbed with pain. I was annoyed. I was uncomfortable. I was thirsty. My lips were parched. My tongue felt like a piece of dry cotton, and my temples throbbed with memories of nightmarish dreams. I knew that I was alive because it hurt too much to be dead. Finally, a nurse, a sweet young thing named Teresa, from Mexico City, came and took compassion on me. She rubbed a cold, wet cloth across my forehead and moistened my lips with a few drops of water. It was like encountering an angel from an oasis after days of walking through the desert.

"Mas, mas agua por favor," (more, more water please), I pleaded.

"No more until tomorrow," she said, and vanished.

I tried burying my head under the pillow in order to muffle the sounds of the unhappy child across the room. The moans of the mother echoed the misery that I was feeling. Tomorrow, I thought, it will be better. If only I can survive until tomorrow.

Tomorrow was better. I received my first bit of nourishment, a cup of tea, chamomile tea, (in Spanish, te de manzanilla) slightly sweetened with sugar. I grew to love my chamomile tea and drank it three to four times a day during my stay in the hospital.

Hilda loved teasing me about the tea. She would ask in Spanish "Quieres te?" (do you want tea?)

I would respond yes, I want tea. "Quiero te"

"No" she would say, "you must say: "Te quiero", which means not "I want tea" but "I love you."

Only when I would finally give in to her game and say "Te quiero" would she bring the tea.

On the morning of the day following the operation, Elsa came to visit. She offered to be my secretary and let me dictate a long and carefully worded letter to my mother explaining all that had happened and asking for her to send money by telegraph, so I could pay the expenses of the hospital. Dr. Vallarino graciously had offered not to charge for his services.

Esther and Pompeyo had seen to it that Elsa had had a chance to visit some of the sites of Mexico. Now, she would be leaving in a few days to return alone to Chicago. I would need to remain a little longer before I could be able to travel.

As I was about to leave the hospital, Dr. Vallarino proudly announced that he had a special gift for me. He handed me a small bottle containing my appendix. "It is your souvenir." He said with a chuckle.

I return to the hotel where I had first stayed and remained there another five days before taking the bus back to Chicago with Pompeyo. Esther would follow after spending a few more days with her family.

I pondered what to do with the special trophy which Dr. Vallarino had bestowed on me. I did not want to carry it home. I couldn't bring myself to just throw it away. Then, in a moment of mischievous play, I decided to leave it in one of the bureau drawers in my hotel room, there to be discovered by an inquisitive chamber maid or unsuspecting guest.

And so, I can truthfully say that there will always be a part of me in old Mexico.

CHAPTER 6 — MISSION IMPOSSIBLE

It was early 1957, about a year and a half after I'd completed my undergraduate degree at Northwestern University's School of Speech. I had no plans to return to college.

Then, a friend told me about a small American college, located on the outskirts of Mexico City. Accredited as a member of the Southern Association of colleges and universities, it offered a graduate program in Latin American Studies, and tuition costs were reasonable. Tucked in the hills just 16 kilometers west of the capital on the road to Toluca, it sounded inviting. It was a way for me to get out of Chicago and back to Mexico.

The school was called Mexico City College. Later, it was moved to the city of Cholula in the state of Puebla, and its name was changed to La Universidad de Las Americas.

Getting myself there and enrolled as a graduate student was the challenge. First, I had to get accepted by the college. That proved to be the easiest part.

In the spring of 1957, I made a trip to Mexico to visit the campus and arrange for my enrollment for the fall. I also arranged with Raul to board with him and his family during my first few months there while attending school.

Back in Chicago, I contacted the Blind Service Association, a local charitable organization with whom I had been acquainted for over seven years. BSA had provided me and scores of other blind students with countless hours of volunteer reading assistance during my undergraduate years at Northwestern and Wright Jr. College. They also provided free canes, braille paper, slates and styluses (for writing braille), and hosted a number of free dinners and parties throughout the year, particularly around Thanksgiving and Christmas. In addition, BSA awarded a limited number of scholarships to specially deserving students with financial need going on to graduate study. It was my hope to persuade the members of the Scholarship Committee of the merits of my plan to study in Mexico.

Their response to my application was encouraging but hesitant. Since they had never before sponsored a student going abroad to study, they wanted to be sure that their decision was a wise one.

To show evidence of my resolve and confidence of success, I committed to go it alone for the first 3 months or school trimester. If I did well, which I fully expected to do, I would ask for their assistance to remain there in school for the balance of the school year. They approved this plan.

Next, I had to figure out how to raise the money to pay for my train ticket to Mexico and to cover my tuition and living expenses during those first 3 months. My part-time job at Radio Station WEAW, hosting a weekly half-hour Latin American music show, wasn't going to generate very much income. Even if I did manage to get more sponsors for my program, I could expect to receive only about $100 a month in commissions.

Through my mom's help, I was able to get another job working evenings as a telephone solicitor for a small heating and air conditioning company in Evanston. I was good at it, and the commissions started to roll in. By July, it still looked doubtful that I was going to be able to amass the nearly $1,000 which I estimated I would need.

Enter Norman. He called himself a cook, but he was more than that. He had a great appreciation for food — how to make it and how to enjoy it. I first met Norman when he rented the extra bedroom next to mine in our converted attic in our house on Lawndale Avenue. Norman was about 12 years my senior, about 6 ft. tall, and weighed in the best of times around 240 lbs. That was his biggest challenge, keeping down his weight. It was particularly hard because of how much he loved to eat, and what he loved to eat — ice cream shakes, French fries, steak and potatoes with lots of gravy, bacon and eggs, hot chocolate with whipped cream.

Norm loved going to those all-night drive-in restaurants so popular back in the 50's. Getting off work around 1 a.m., he'd swing by the house to pick me up and we'd go out for coffee or hot chocolate and some stimulating intellectual conversations. Our favorite topics were philosophy, literature, paranormal phenomena, the possibility of extra-terrestrial life, and religion.

Although he had only a high school education, Norman loved the quest for knowledge. He read a great deal and held a deep respect for institutions of higher learning. He even took a couple of courses in English at Lake Forest College.

No doubt it was in part because of this high regard for the pursuit of knowledge that he offered to help me financially when I revealed my desire to enroll in a college in Mexico City. It was to be a loan. For each of the first five months that I would be there, Norman committed to mail me a money order for $90.00. Because of the favorable rate of exchange of pesos to dollars and my boarding with Raul and his family, I calculated that this would be quite adequate to cover my personal and living expenses. A friend in need is a friend indeed. Even though I was able years later to pay Norman back in full, I will always be indebted to him for giving me that hand up when I needed it most.

Now everything was in place. September came, and off I went on my long train ride to Mexico, carrying with me, among other things, a 40 pound manual Royal typewriter, which I planned to use for typing term papers and letters back home.

All went well my first couple of months. I took one course in commercial business writing in Spanish and two classes in economics, which were required for my major.

My economics instructor was young and seemed inexperienced at lecturing. His classes consisted almost exclusively of his reading verbatim from the textbook, and our questions were answered with a curt "We'll get to that later."

The material, though rather dry, seemed easy enough to comprehend. Thus, I was totally unprepared for the shock when I got a grade of C on both my midterm exams in economics. I felt certain that I knew the material better than that. What was worse, I was to forward copies of my grades to the Scholarship Committee at Blind Service Association back in Chicago. It would not bode well for my chances of obtaining a scholarship for them to see me doing only "average" work.

I decided to talk with the instructor. I asked him: "Why did I do so poorly?".

"I always grade low on midterm exams." He explained. "I can assure you that you will come out better on the final."

47

But I wasn't so certain. I told him the reason for my concern, that I was under consideration for a scholarship and was supposed to inform the scholarship committee back in Chicago of my midterm progress. These C's might jeopardize my chances of being favorably considered.

To my surprise, he offered to do a most unusual thing. He offered to write a note to the scholarship committee clarifying my C grades and recommend they hold their judgment of my academic performance until after seeing my final grades for the two courses. True to his word, he wrote the note and I mailed it along with a copy of my grades to BSA. I was amazed yet very pleased that he would do this for me. Also true to his prediction, I received B's as my final grades in both of his classes.

I was genuinely relieved and sincerely grateful until I learned later from some of my fellow students that this instructor was "selling" grades to those willing to pay the price. Darn! I thought, I could have bought for myself a couple of A's.

When school administrators became aware of what was happening, he was summarily fired. Later it was learned that he was not a genuine professor at all. He had duped the college, having falsified his credentials and references. It was a tremendous scandal and embarrassment for the college.

What was worse was that his chicanery had almost irrevocably altered my life's path. Fortunately, however, my two B's in Economics and A in Spanish satisfied BSA's scholarship committee, and I was granted the financial assistance which made it possible for me to remain in college in Mexico.

CHAPTER 7—RAUL'S PLACE

Raul's place was located in one of the poorest and oldest sections of the city. A small apartment at Plaza de San Lazaro #9, Interior 22, it was about 3 miles east of the "Zocalo" or main square.

There were 50 or 60 families who lived in the complex. All the apartments faced on to a large patio or courtyard. The courtyard served as a safe playground for the children, a place to exchange gossip with neighbors, and a wonderful spot for numerous fiestas, celebrations and Christmas posadas.

It was like a small community. Everyone knew everyone else's business. Access to the complex was through a large iron door which was shut tight and locked after dark to protect the residents. If you came home late, you had to pound on the door to wake up the watchman, identify yourself as a resident and then give him a few coins for disturbing his sleep.

Raul's place was a two-room apartment on the second floor. One room served as the living area, dining-room and bedroom for his wife and three children. The other, a smaller room with two beds, was where Raul and I slept. A tiny kitchen at the entranceway contained a sink and two-burner butane stove. Next to the kitchen was the toilet. It had no water tank. After using it, you had to fill up a bucket with water at the sink and pour it down the toilet. It was like an inside outhouse.

Despite the somewhat spartan nature of these accommodations, I was sincerely grateful to Raul for opening up his home to me as a friend and student who had to live on an extremely limited budget.

Raul's family welcomed me warmly into their household. It consisted of his young wife, Catarina, and their children, Irma, Neomi and Cesar. They ranged in age from 9 to 6. Irma and Cesar were visually impaired like their father. I became especially close to 9-year-old Irma. I walked with her to the candy store on Sunday afternoons and told her bedtime stories about princes and princesses when she found it hard to go to sleep.

Some 35 years later, Irma and her British husband, Charlie, came to visit us in San Antonio. Recalling my story-telling talent, she commented: "You know I never stayed awake long enough to hear how those stories of yours ended."

"Well," I admitted, "I don't know how they ended either. I just made them up as I went along." We both laughed.

Raul struggled to support his family, playing the piano for a church congregation on Sundays and giving therapeutic massages to occasional clients during the week. His earnings rarely were more than 50 pesos a week, about 4 dollars. Music and massage therapy were the two principle vocations taught at the Escuela Nacional Para Ciegos (National School for the Blind) in Mexico City where Raul was educated. These were the careers which most blind persons in Mexico followed.

Raul's mother, who lived next door with his sister Celia and her family, did most of the marketing and most of the cooking. My weekly contribution to the household budget helped assure that we had plentiful if simple food at every meal. I learned to eat a lot of new and unusual dishes. Some I learned to love, like fresh papaya with lime juice, atole (a beverage made from rice or corn flour and served hot), and chongos (a delicious dessert made from curdled milk.

Others I really had to struggle with, like nopales (stewed cactus), cilantro (a pungent herb used to season many typical dishes), and camote (sweet potatoes) served at breakfast.

Besides being a versatile and resourceful cook, Raul's mother was an excellent domino player. Prior to my going to Mexico, I thought the only thing you did with dominoes was to see how many you could stack before they would topple over. During my 9 months' stay with Raul, I discovered the fun and challenge of trying to outguess your opponents and play the pieces that would force them to pass and allow you to win. Fortified with a bottle of rum and a pitcher of slightly sweetened lime water, Raul, his mother, and I held nightly seminars until 2 or 3 a.m. on the art of playing dominoes. At first, as a novice, I was quite resigned to losing. But as the months wore on, Raul's mother continued to beat us soundly every time.

Finally, after about six months, I asked Raul: "When will we get good enough to beat your mother?"

His answer "nunca" (never). "She always wins." And indeed she did.

Sunday mornings are my favorite time to sleep in. But at Raul's place, this was not easy to do. The womenfolk were up at sunrise doing the cleaning and laundry. Windows were thrown open wide to let in the fresh air. Radios came on full blast, and there was a large, green and yellow parrot, belonging to one of our neighbors, who loved to sing along with the music.

Although Raul had no vision at all, he insisted on traveling the streets of Mexico City without the use of a cane or dog guide. It was amazing to me how he managed to travel so confidently about the city. Boarding buses and crossing busy intersections, he relied on his wits and the occasional help from passersby. He was an excellent and resourceful guide. No matter where I needed to go, Raul knew the right buses to take to get us there. He taught me to pay attention to landmarks that you could smell or hear, like a bakery, a fruit stand or a music store. He instructed me in the proper phrases to use to ask for help in crossing a street and how to get a bus driver's cooperation to let us know when to get off.

Thanks to Raul I, too, learned to travel with confidence throughout the capital and continued to use his techniques during my 17 years there. Strangely, I never did much use the new metro (subway system) which was built in the late 60's. Perhaps it was because Raul was not there to show me how.

With Raul's help I also learned about the wide variety of excellent Mexican beer—Dos X, Carta Blanca, Bohemia, Corona, Superior, Tecate (at the time the only beer in a can), and Victoria. This last was considered the beer of bricklayers because it was dark, bitter, and inexpensive. It cost 65 centavos the bottle, (about a nickel in U.S. money). Because of its price, it was also our favorite.

Raul and I spent a lot of time together, especially evenings and weekends. We enjoyed going to parties, visiting with his relatives, playing dominoes, or debating social issues with his blind musician friends. During these gatherings I became aware of how common it was to see Raul and his friends casually sharing one or more marijuana cigarettes. It was their moment of escape from the despair of economic privation, a communion of fellowship and fraternal understanding. Although I declined their invitations to join in, I was never criticized or pressured to do so. Their attitude was, if he says no, that means more for us.

It was while staying at Raul's place that I had my first and only taste of turtle soup. It wasn't actually in his home but at a small restaurant which we frequented near the National School for the Blind. In general, the meals we took at this family-owned restaurant were good and very reasonable. The five-course meal consisted of a pasta soup, followed by a plate of rice with saffron or sweet peas. Then the main meat course which might be pork with squash, stewed chicken and vegetables or a small grilled ministeak. This would be followed by a plate of frijoles (boiled or refried beans) and then dessert of fruit or ice cream. A bottle of apple or lemon soda and a small cup of black coffee finished off the meal. All this for the price of about 50 cents U.S.

On this occasion, instead of the pasta soup, they offered turtle soup. Raul chose consome instead. I had never tasted turtle soup before and thought it would be fun to try. It reminded me somewhat of seafood chowder back in Chicago. But the turtle meat was apparently spoiled.

By evening, I had excruciating stomach pains and a severe case of diarrhea and vomiting. As I made my frequent trips to the bathroom, I didn't know whether to sit down or lean over.

By morning, I was so weak from loss of fluid that I could hardly walk. I thought that I was going to die.

Raul decided that I needed to see a doctor. This meant getting up, getting dressed, and going to the doctor. His doctor did not make house calls.

Raul practically had to carry me down the stairs to the taxi. My legs were like jelly. My head was swimming. Voices came to me sounding muffled and strangely distant. All I could think about was how soon could I get back to my bed and lie down.

Finally, we arrived at the doctor's place. His office was up on the second floor. Again, Raul wrapped his big bear-like arms around me and virtually carried me up the stairs and into the doctor's office. There, I slumped into a chair.

Raul described my symptoms and the origin of my problem to the doctor, an old man with a frail voice. He listened quietly, then approached me, speaking softly and reassuringly. Asking me to lean back in my chair he Pplaced his hands on my abdomen and gently applied a little pressure here and a little there, observing my responses, which were mostly feeble groans. Turning to Raul, he confirmed the diagnosis of food poisoning.

Next he stepped to a wall of shelves containing numerous bottles, jars, jugs and vessels. Dimly I heard him transferring the contents from one vessel to another. He then approached Raul, handing him two bottles containing different colored sugar pills. No penicillin, no sulfur drugs, this was homeopathy. I had heard about "natural" medicine, but I had never been exposed to it. Well I was going to be now. And I was going to find out first-hand just how effective it was.

The doctor gave Raul careful instructions on which pills I was to take, when, and what I was and was not to eat and drink. Addressing me, he assured "you will be as good as new in 3 to 4 days."

I had my doubts.

Raul managed to get me back down the stairs, into a taxi and back home, where I collapsed into my bed exhausted. Raul's mother made sure I followed the doctor's instructions to the letter—taking ten of the pink pills now, ten of the blue ones an hour from now, and my diet of chicken broth, camomile tea and Jell-O.

It worked. By the third day I was nearly fully recovered, a few pounds lighter but ready to take Raul's mother on in another domino game.

Were the sugar pills that effective or had my body's natural defenses finally just prevailed? I don't really know. Perhaps both. What I can say is after that experience, I lost my taste for turtle soup.

Raul loved life and he cared about people deeply. His death ten years later on his 40th birthday was a tragically cruel statement of the poverty in which he lived. He died an agonizing death, consuming as he had done so many times before, a taco, an ordinary taco from a street vendor whose habits of sanitation left much to be desired. The resulting food poisoning weakened and wasted away the Goliath frame, and because of inadequate or inappropriate medical attention, he finally succumbed to an early demise.

Time and circumstance had caused us to drift apart. So, I was deeply shocked and saddened when I learned of his death. Yet, it was, regretably, not so unusual an occurrence among Mexico City's masses of poor.

CHAPTER 8 — MUSIC AS YOU LIKE IT

It was while living at Raul's place that I began listening to the English language radio programs broadcast over station XEL, Radio Capital. I thought to myself, I can do that. I could work there.

XEL, Radio Capital, was one of some 35 or 40 AM radio stations in Mexico City, with an equal number of FM stations. XEL was the pioneer in English language programming for Mexico City. There was a large population of English-speaking foreigners — Americans, British and Canadians, and a sizable group of other foreign nationals whose second language was English. It was a very loyal and affluent audience.

These programs were also directed to an even larger audience of Mexicans who wished to learn English. Secretaries could earn 20 to 50% more if they were bilingual. Executives could hope to be promoted from junior executive to senior executives if they were fluent in English. Thus, from an economic standpoint, the incentive for Mexicans to learn English was very strong.

Together, these groups represented a sizable audience for XEL, Radio Capital, which offered five hours a day in English,

1-1/2 hours in the morning and 3-1/2 hours in the evening, plus 13 hours a day in Spanish.

In early December, I visited the station and met with Ingeniero Ignacio Diaz, the tall, affable, mid-40ish technical director who spoke very fluent and cultured English. I told him about my 3 years of experience with Station WEAW in Evanston Illinois and my degree in speech from Northwestern University. He was impressed. He said that although they had no need for additional English speaking announcers at this time, he would speak with the owner Don Fidel Hernandez about me. I was so eager to get back behind a microphone that I offered to work as a volunteer to show what I could do.

About a week later, I was given the chance. Ingeniero Diaz asked if I was interested in doing a classical music show, a one-hour program on Sunday nights from 9 to 10 p.m. I said, sure! Borrowing the name from one of my favorite plays by Shakespeare, I titled the program "Music As You Like It". For my signature theme I selected the overture to "Swan Lake".

XEL, Radio Capital, I discovered, had a very limited library of classical music albums, and what records there were, were pretty scratchy. Nevertheless, the audience seemed to enjoy the program, and it gave me a foot in the door.

About two months after I had been doing the program, without pay, I learned from another American announcer that he was being paid for the hour that I worked. When I inquired about this, the station agreed to put me on the payroll, and I began earning all of 6.50 pesos (ninety cents) for the hour. (the exchange rate at that time was 8.65 to the dollar).

I enjoyed doing the show and enjoyed even more talking with listeners by telephone. As some of the American announcers moved on, more time became available, and I was asked to do more programs. I loved it. I began working six and seven evenings a week while attending school during the day.

The musical menu we played was everything from international to middle-of-the-road, to popular big-band sounds, to folk music, to jazz, to opera—a little bit of everything. We also had nightly news casts, interview shows, sports, and programs for the ladies.

At one point, I did a live weekly rock-n-roll show with a studio full of amplifiers, electronic guitars, pulsating percussions and wildly enthusiastic teenagers. I didn't know it at the time, but this was a foreshadowing of things to come.

XEL Radio Capital was located, during the first years of my tenure as an English language announcer, at Paseo de la Reforma 400. This is a beautiful, eight-lane, Champs Elissez-like avenue bordered by tall trees and floral gardens. Every quarter of a mile there is a beautiful fountain or historical monument—Carlos IV, Christopher Columbus, the Angel of Independence, Diana the Huntress and Simon Bolivar, the great liberator of South America.

During the Christmas season, it was traditional that this beautiful avenue would be adorned with a crisscross of colored lights and decorations—wise men, angels, reindeer, Santa Claus, pinatas and more. It was a site to behold, one which caused passing motorists to pause and marvel and tourists to return at this special time of the year for snapshot souvenirs.

Much of the tourism of Mexico City revolved around the Paseo de la Reforma—beautiful modern hotels, fashionable boutiques, elegant restaurants, and of course the Castle of Chapultepec.

Some of my fondest memories are of lingering walks along the beautiful Paseo. There was at once both a feeling of freedom and of excitement. The broad floral gardens which lined the thoroughfare invited one to promenade. There were portly businessmen wearing too much after-shave awaiting their turn for a shine of shoes. There were haughty debutantes strolling with their mamas, gazing down at the ground and at the people. There were American tourists with cameras slung over shoulder, straw hat on head, doling out Roosevelt dimes to hungry urchins with hands extended. There were hookers and hawkers and hospital workers, nurses and teachers and nuns. There were students whose carefree, raucous laughter bespoke the confidence and the naivete of their youth. And there were peasant Indian women wrapped in their shawls whose stoicism and poverty made not a single sound. All of Mexico was here in the Paseo, all of the strata of life—the ugly, the sad, and the beautiful.

XEL Radio Capital was located just across from the Golden Angel of Independence. It was this same angel which fell during the strong earthquake which hit the city in June of 1957, just 3 months before I arrived. Some residents claimed that the angel was trying to seduce the goddess Diana a half mile up the thoroughfare and fell head over heels for her. In any event, the noble angel was returned to his perch just a few months after the tumble, no doubt with a strong admonition from the archbishop.

The studios of Radio Capital looked out upon this monument to independence from the seventh floor. It was, fortunately, a sturdy building. I recall spending many a rocky moment during smaller earthquakes feeling the building sway as I calmly announced the upcoming record. Sometimes, as a result of the quake, the power would fail, and we'd go off the air. When we returned, it would be with a polite excuse to the audience: "Sorry we were gone but now we're back." It was absolutely forbidden to report the actual occurrence of an earthquake while in progress. One newscaster had daringly chosen to do this during the 1957 quake and his license was revoked for two years.

Ignoring earthquakes was part of the national penchant for ignoring all types of bad news. I learned a lot about the Latin yearning to escape from sadness, disappointment and reality. The men used marijuana, tequila, and women. The women, for the most part, listened to soap operas, read romantic novels and complained to one another.

Being a "locutor", (an announcer) for a radio station in Mexico, meant that you had to be licensed by the Secretaria de Educacion (Secretariat of Education). To obtain a license, you had to study for and pass an exam in Spanish, provide two recent photographs and pay a licensing fee. Foreigners could obtain only temporary or "guest" licenses, which had to be renewed every 90 days. This was a bit of a nuisance. After working for more than five years, I was finally allowed by the Secretary of Education to renew it only twice a year.

Getting a job as an announcer in Mexico was more a matter of who you knew rather than what you knew. Indeed, some of the announcers at the larger, more prestigious stations such as Pedro Ferris, Paco Malgesto and Ken Smith were true professionals, well respected, with great talent and abilities. But most of the locutores were just guys with deep voices who loved to talk and could read a couple of pages of news copy and/or a commercial without making too many fluffs.

Being a locutor gave one a certain status with the general public and a special appeal with the opposite sex. The majority of the locutores I knew were not the least bit hesitant to take full advantage of it. This was definitely true with the locutores at XEL Radio Capital. Though married, most had a girlfriend or two or three. Any female listener who called in was a candidate for seductive persuasion over the phone by the locutor who took the call. Some were just looking for titillating sexual conversation, while others accepted the locutor's invitation for a rendezvous. Either way, my colleagues were always happy to oblige.

CHAPTER 9 – LOST AND FOUND

The day I lost my wrist watch was the day I met the girl who was to become my wife.

During the 1950's, Mexico City College was one of the favorite places for Korean veterans on the GI bill to go to college. U.S. dollars went a lot further. Academically, classes were fairly easy. The climate was beautiful and so were the senoritas.

During the spring quarter of 1958 a fellow student told me of an announcement on the college bulletin board. It read: "Wanted! Ten American students to work part-time, two hours a week, as discussion leaders for a group of Mexican students learning conversational English at Mexico City College's Business & Commercial campus."

This sounded like it could be fun and a chance to pick up some extra cash. I applied and was selected as one of the ten. The campus was located in the Colonia Roma, just a short bus ride from XEL Radio Capital. I had little trouble finding my way there.

We met in a large open room full of tables. During the day the room was used as the cafeteria. There were perhaps 60 Mexican students, 90% female, and ten of us Americans. We sat together in small groups of 6 to 8, and conversed in English for the next two hours. We got paid 20 pesos ($2.50 U.S.) and hour. It was the easiest and most enjoyable job I have ever had.

In my group there was one guy and 7 lovely young senoritas—all very bright and very eager to practice their English. One of the brightest was a petite, dark-eyed girl of 18 named Diana. She was a little more reserved than the rest. You might even say aloof. Perhaps that's what caught my attention. She didn't giggle and gush over the American boys like her companions. She had an air of self-confidence and independence which I found intriguing.

Conversation flowed easily. We talked about the differing customs in our two countries, about popular favorite songs and artists and about the meaning of words and idiomatic expressions. The two hours were up before we knew it. I didn't know it then, but I had just met my wife to be.

As I boarded my bus to go home I checked my Gotham braille watch which had been given to me 8 years earlier by a southside Chicago Kiwanis club. It was just past 9 o'clock. I treasured that timepiece. It was my first braille watch. It was extremely durable, in an all-steel case, and had a handsome Spidel band.

Leaving the bus at my stop and walking the three blocks to Raul's place, I reflected back on the delightful evening I had just spent. The night was unusually quiet. Strangely absent were the familiar and reassuring night whistles of the self-appointed neighborhood sentinels, who alerted one another of the unwelcome approach of the police or of strangers.

As I walked past the neighborhood cantina, about a half block from my destination, two figures suddenly emerged from the shadows. One grabbed me from behind, wrapping both arms around my neck, pulling me backwards off balance. My cane went flying in one direction, and a braille book I was carrying flew in another. At first, I thought perhaps it was a friend of Raul's or mine engaging in some friendly horseplay. As I struggled to catch my fall with one hand and tried to loosen his grip with the other, his companion reached in and grabbed my wristwatch, twisting it so that the pin holding the band snapped. I don't know if he had a weapon. Not a word was spoken. It was all over in a matter of seconds.

I was dazed and angry. As they ran off, I futilely yelled after them in Spanish, "The watch will be of no use to you."

Hearing the fracas, two men emerged from the cantina. One helped me to my feet while the other took chase after the thieves, but to no avail. They were swifter of foot and quickly disappeared into the night.

When I got to Raul's place, I was reluctant to tell him what had happened. I was too humiliated and embarrassed. But he learned the truth a couple of days later from his underworld friends. By then it was too late to recover my watch. It had changed hands too many times. Raul commented that if I had told him of the incident that same evening, his friends might indeed have gotten it back. I didn't trust enough.

About a week later, Raul told me that one of my assailants had been seriously injured in a fight. "God punished him." Raul said simply.

God had also introduced me to a beautiful life companion.

CHAPTER 10—MOVING UP TOWN

I suppose it was partly because of my experience of being mugged and having my watch stolen in Raul's neighborhood, and partly because I was now working six nights a week at Radio Capital that I decided it was time to move up town. I checked with the college's housing office, and they gave me a referral to an address on Rio Ebro in Colonia Cuauhtemoc. It was just two blocks from the Paseo de La Reforma and only 3 blocks from the angel. It seemed perfect. I'd be able to walk to and from to work at Radio Capital and could catch the bus in the morning on La Reforma up to the college.

The landlady, La Senora of the house was a short, middle-aged, no-nonsense woman married to a local police chief. I learned that there were three other students, two Americans and one from Spain, presently boarding with this family. Our quarters were located on the second floor, which we were obliged to reach by climbing up an outside metal staircase. Except for the first day, when I met La Senora, none of us was ever invited into the house to be part of the family, to watch television or simply to sit and talk. The only times we came into the dining-room were to take our two meals each day. Those meals, though nourishing, were rather scant for hungry young men. And there were no seconds. It was quite a change for me from the warm hospitality, family atmosphere and plentiful food which I had experienced at Raul's place. La Senora was a businesswoman. She had one motive in mind for taking in student borders: It was to make money.

I had never before eaten an orange peel. But one day, while standing on the small balcony outside our rooms, a young girl from next door started a conversation with me. She asked, "Do you like candied orange peals?"

"I've don't think I've ever eaten one." I replied.

"Then, I'll send you one to try." She said. And she did. Her maid brought it to me. It was a complete orange peal. I marveled at how it had been kept in tact. I tasted it. It was delicious. Very sweet. I finished it all, selfishly not sharing any of it with my roommates.

I went out on the balcony several afternoons after that hoping to have another conversation with the young lady and to thank her for the treat. But she never appeared.

Despite its convenient location, I decided, after a couple of months, it was time to make another move. One of the other students staying there was an American named Paul Gaboriault. Paul was from the Northeast, from Vermont. He was quite proud of his French Canadian ancestry and delighted in telling people his full name which was Paul Henri

Gaboriault de la Tour de la Pan. Despite his somewhat pompous nature, Paul and I struck up a friendship. He, too, was ready to look for a more suitable place where we could have more space and more freedom.

At the end of the spring semester, I planned to go back to Chicago for a month's vacation during the summer. Paul, however, was going to stay in Mexico. He agreed to look around for our new quarters.

When I returned, he showed me what he had found. It was a comfortable two-room place above a restaurant on Calle Lieja, just a half block from the Diana fountain. This would put me some six blocks from Radio Capital. I could easily walk it in ten minutes or take a "pesero", one of the collective taxis, which ran regularly up and down La Reforma and cost just one peso.

Our new quarters consisted of a small anteroom or reception area with a desk and a couple of chairs. This connected with a large bedroom with two double beds, two dressers, two bureaus and a large closet. One inconvenience was that we did not have a private bathroom. We had to go down the hall and share the facilities with a half dozen other tenants. It was somewhat like living again at the YMCA. But, for us it worked well. The restaurant downstairs offered good inexpensive meals.

One of the special memories I have of our stay at Lieja was Paul reading to me Bram Stoker's 19th century thriller, Dracula. We'd race home from school, eat lunch, do our class assignments and then settle in for a couple of scary chapters with the Count. Paul was an excellent reader and really made the characters come alive. I loved reading ghost stories when I was a kid, and this was the ultimate of all ghost stories.

After living at Lieja for about three months, Paul proposed combining our financial resources with another classmate and renting a real apartment. The place he had in mind was in a fashionable section of Mexico City called Las Lomas, a lovely residential area of rolling hills along the Paseo de la Reforma, just two miles west of beautiful Chapultepec Park. Many Americans, including the U.S. ambassador and other foreign nationals, either rented or owned large Spanish-style residences there.

The second-floor apartment had one large master bedroom, a smaller bedroom, bathroom, living-room/dining-room combination, and a fully equipped kitchen. We figured that by cooking some of our own meals, we could save money. We could have friends over to visit. We could have parties. And, with three of us sharing the rent, Paul and I would actually be paying less than what we were paying at Lieja. Our new roommate was a fellow from Nicaragua named Carlos. He

73

chose the separate small bedroom and paid a little more for the privacy.

With New Year's Eve just a couple of weeks away, we decided to organize a party. We would invite a bunch of girls and serve a special vodka punch and have a great time. Well, all the girls we asked at school already had plans and parties to go to. Since I had made friends with a couple of the girls at the bank where I cashed my checks, I took a chance and invited them. To my surprise and delight they accepted.

Paul and I went to the market and purchased a large assortment of fruit. Next, we stopped at the liquor store and picked up a bottle of cheap vodka. Neither of us were vodka drinkers, but we had heard that when you mix vodka with fruit juice, you can hardly tell it's there. We bought a large bottle, the least expensive we could find. (Why spend more than you have to to get your guests feeling good?)

Back at the apartment, we cut and squeezed limes, oranges, pineapples, and tangerines. We added sugar and then the vodka. We set out bowls with chips and nuts. We placed our one small radio on the mantle, tuned to some lively dance music, and waited.

At 8 o'clock sharp the two girls from the bank arrived. They were definitely dressed for a party in their velvet and satin and sequins. We felt embarrassed in our casual clothes.

They looked around expectantly, wondering I'm sure where the rest of the people were. But it was just Carlos, Paul and I.

Determined to make our guests enjoy themselves, we turned the radio a bit louder and brought on our very special punch. We hadn't yet tasted it ourselves. What a mistake that was. It was dreadful. The cheap vodka we'd used had a bitter after-taste and completely overpowered the flavors of the fruit juices.

After about a half hour of polite strained conversation, the girls told us they had to leave. Their families, they said, were expecting them back home. We were too embarrassed to protest. It was almost with relief that we said our good-byes at the door and thanked them for coming.

The evening was a bust. Here it was New Year's Eve. We had two beautiful companions ready to go party, and there wasn't any party. We had no money to take them anywhere, and our special New Year's punch was undrinkable. We poured the punch down the toilet, picked up the chips and nuts and turned off the radio.

"So now what do we do?" I asked.

"Beats me." replied Carlos. "One thing I know, we'll never see those chicks again. Hey, listen, where's that music coming from?"

"Sounds like from downstairs." Paul said.

"Sounds like a real party." Carlos added.

"Well, what say we go investigate?" I suggested.

And so we did. The apartment downstairs and across the hall were jam packed with people dancing, drinking and having a good ole time. Pushing our way in through the open door, we were amazed to see the two lovely senoritas from the bank who had just left our apartment downcast and demure minutes earlier having the time of their lives dancing to Elvis Presley and "Jailhouse Rock". They saw us, smiled and waved, and went on dancing. After that experience, we learned our lesson: know your booze and have a wider selection on hand.

The apartment's furnishings included a large open cabinet in the dining-room area, just perfect for a bar. Paul dedicated himself to becoming a connoisseur of domestic wines and liquors. It wasn't long before we had stocked our "cantina" bar with a wide assortment of rums, wines and brandies. Many an afternoon and evening, we conducted serious scientific taste tests to determine if we could in fact tell the difference between Bacardi rum Carta de Oro and the more expensive Ron Anejo.

CHAPTER 11 — BLIND TRUST

The career of a radio deejay is a very interesting one. It allows you to get to know all kinds of people, many of whom you only meet by telephone.

During most of my 17 years as a deejay in Mexico City, I worked the late night shift. I often took calls from persons who had problems, some of them quite serious. I talked with runaways, with kids trying to kick their drug habit, and with people contemplating divorce or suicide. There were patients listening from their hospital beds, recovering from an accident or long illness. Many of them were lonely, frightened, unhappy people — people wanting desperately to have someone to talk to, someone to confide in.

I became counselor, psychologist, father-confessor. I took it as a pretty serious responsibility. Mostly, I just tried to listen. Occasionally, I was privileged to be able to help.

There was Madam X who spoke with a decidedly British accent. She loved Eddie Fisher and Frank Sinatra. When we switched to a Top 40 format in 1963, she was quite displeased and stopped listening.

There was Adriana, who wanted the experience of safe sexual arousal over the telephone through the nightly discussion of acts of explicit sex. Her fantasies were sometimes entertaining, sometimes boring.

There was Aki, a young English-speaking Japanese girl who attended the American High School in Mexico City. She idolized the Beatles and would not stand for anyone to criticize her idols, not even in jest.

Aki was one of my most loyal listeners during the four years she lived in Mexico. She would regularly call or send in 15 to 20 requests each week. Ninety-nine percent of them would be songs by the Beatles. Her love was Paul McCartney.

Upon her return to Japan, she wrote to me once or twice a year, sending me lovely cards. Even after my leaving Mexico and Radio Capital, our friendship and correspondence continued. It was so interesting to watch her grow from young impressionable teenager to career-minded woman, to wife, to mother. With the passing of Beatlemania, she switched her allegiance to Peter, Paul and Mary.

In 1995 my wife and I had the delightful experience of visiting Japan and the very special pleasure of meeting Aki in person for the first time. She had divorced, changed careers, and become a freelance translator and interpreter. She had also moved into a new apartment and felt confident that life still held for her many wonderful things. I am certain that it does.

During the ten days we were in Japan, Aki became our self-appointed volunteer interpreter and guide. She did her best to make our visit a truly memorable one. And it was.

Of all my many radio experiences in Mexico, there is one which stands out most in my mind. It involved a young lady named Jackie. Jackie was in her mid 20's. She was bitter, depressed, and full of resentment. She felt that life had dealt her a cruel blow. But it was not until her fifth call that she revealed to me what was troubling her.

About a year earlier, she had been in an automobile accident. As a result, she had lost her sight. She felt cheated by life and angry towards God. I gently asked her what she had done since the accident.

"Nothing, really," she admitted, "just waited and hoped that somehow, some way, some miracle would bring back my sight."

I tried to reassure her that being blind wasn't the worst thing in the world that could happen. I suggested that she needed to prepare herself in the event that the miracle might never come. I talked to her about learning braille and about other services which were available to persons without vision. I suggested that she still could find purpose and meaning in life. Her response was to lash out at me in anger.

"How would you know what it's like to be blind?" she challenged. "It's easy for you to say, It's not so bad. But you haven't been there."

I listened to her tirade with calm compassion, letting her vent her bitterness and anger and fear. And then I said quietly to her:

"Yes, Jackie, I do know what it's like because, you see, I am also blind."

I was not prepared for her reaction. She became even more angry and shouted at me.

"Why do you mock me? Do you think I am stupid? How is it possible that you can be a disc jockey and be blind? You are cruel!" she said, "and you are a liar."

With that, she slammed down the phone, without giving me a chance to respond. I felt awful. I felt frustrated and guilty. Yes, I had told her the truth, but perhaps I should have waited, or told it to her differently. I had gambled that my revelation would shock her out of her state of self-pity. Instead, it had enraged her.

Did she believe me? Would she call back? I wondered, had I lost the chance to help someone in distress.

I slept very restlessly that night. All through the next day Jackie's words kept coming back to me. "You are cruel!"

Was I, in fact, truly insensitive to her anguish? I have lived with blindness all of my life and have accepted its inconveniences. Perhaps, because of this, I was not able to understand or feel the deep fear and the sense of helplessness and loss which she was experiencing. It has to be a lot harder, I suppose, for someone who has sight suddenly to lose it. For many loss of sight means loss of independence, loss of self-confidence, even loss of the desire to live. So many of our daily routine activities seem to depend upon our ability to see — selecting what clothes we'll wear, reading the newspaper, pouring a cup of coffee, going to work, shopping at the mall, paying bills, watching tv — so many things. To a sighted person, it seems impossible to imagine being able to do these things without sight. But they can be done, perhaps some of them in slightly different ways, but they can be done. Of course, Jackie didn't know this.

The next night I waited and hoped and prayed that she would call back. About an hour into the program, her call came. She was calmer now.

"Why did you tell me last night that you were blind?" she asked.

"Because I am," I said matter-of-factly.

"But, but you can't be. You don't sound blind, I mean," she stammered.

81

"Well, you don't sound blind either," I replied. We both laughed. "If you want to check it out", I offered, "You can call the station manager tomorrow and ask him."

"But how is it possible? How can you be working if you are blind?" she asked.

I explained to her that being blind did not mean being void of talent or ability. I told her there are blind lawyers, blind teachers, blind musicians—blind people doing a lot of different jobs.

"Hey Jackie, absence of sight doesn't necessarily mean absence of intelligence or talent." I quipped.

I shared with her about my schooling and work activities. I told her that I was nearing completion of a Master's degree in economics at the local American university, that I was married and had children, all of them sighted. I suggested that she too could aspire to do many things even if her sight never returned.

She listened attentively, wanting to believe but still filled with doubt. We talked long that night, and the next, and the next. In fact, over the next several weeks she called every evening. We talked at length about her fear of blindness and about those things she still could do without sight. A warm bond of trust was building between us. I felt tremendous satisfaction that perhaps I was helping to make a difference, a positive difference, in Jackie's attitude and outlook on life.

And then, one night, there it was, the promise of a miracle! Her uncle in California had written to her family and told them of a new medical procedure that perhaps, just perhaps, could restore Jackie's vision.

She was to fly to Los Angeles and enter the hospital to have the operation within a couple of weeks. But now she was filled with a new sense of apprehension and fear. She didn't know if she should go through with it. What if it didn't work? What if she remained blind, or worse? She asked me for my advice.

"Take the chance", I told her. "Don't count on it. If it worked, it'll be a blessing from Heaven. If it doesn't, it's God's will, and you can still have a happy and productive life."

She seemed reassured. We discussed the operation a lot over the next several days. Finally, she made up her mind. She would go ahead with it.

I next heard from her about a week later. It was the eve of her departure for California.

"Oh, thank you Larry for giving me the courage to go and I promise to call you just as soon as I return to let you know how it turned out."

"Good luck, Jackie." I said.

The waiting was awful. What if something went wrong? What if there were complications? Here I was urging her to go through with a major operation, about which I knew very little. Who was I anyway to be giving medical advice on so important a decision to someone I didn't even really know?

About three weeks later, I received her call.

"Hello Larry, this is Jackie."

My heart leaped with excitement. "Yes, Jackie. How are you?" I tried to keep my voice calm, but the anticipation was killing me. "I've been wondering about you. How did it go?"

"I can see again," she said.

There were goose bumps all over my body. I wanted to cheer. I felt great joy for her and, at the same time, a tremendous sense of relief. Thank God! I thought to myself. "How wonderful for you Jackie," I said.

"And I want to thank you Larry. I really want to thank you." she repeated.

"For what?" I asked.

"For giving me the courage to take the chance—for being there for me when I needed someone."

"You don't have to thank me for anything, Jackie", I replied. "I'm just so very happy it all worked out for you."

"Yes, I'm happy too," she said, "and I'd like the chance to tell you so in person."

I was certainly curious to meet this young woman whom I had known for over 4 months, only by telephone. How would she behave now that we no longer had a common bond? We were now different. She could see.

We agreed to meet the following afternoon for a cup of coffee. She came to my office around 4 o'clock. We walked to Sanborns restaurant, on the Reforma, back then a popular spot for American tourists. We talked for about an hour. I learned that Jackie was born in Mexico City of Jewish parents. She described herself as medium tall, about five-foot five, and slender, with light brown shoulder-length hair and hazel eyes. She wore very thick glasses, explaining that she would have to wear them at least for the next three months while her eyes became reaccustomed. She told me about the operation and how excited and thrilled her family was over her regaining her sight. She was thrilled too, of course. Now she could get on with her life. Her blindness had been a dark and frightening interlude, like a bad dream. But now it was over. Her life had been healed.

Somehow I felt we were now two strangers. The dramatic crisis of recent months which had brought us together was now past. The intense emotional bond which had existed between us melted away. She no longer needed my help, my support, my counsel.

We left the restaurant and stood quietly among the flowered gardens along the Paseo de La Reforma. She told me that she was engaged to be married. I wished her luck and happiness. We said our good-byes with a silent embrace, and I knew somehow that this was a final farewell.

I never heard from Jackie again. But, it had been an extraordinary experience, a special opportunity to help another human being in time of need. It has remained one of the most cherished memories of my broadcasting career.

CHAPTER 12—WEDDING BELLS

Diana and I had been going together for about ten months. Our courtship involved long walks in the early evenings, during which we sang songs and had wonderful conversations. We also enjoyed going to the movies. There was one Saturday when we went to three full-length feature films at three different movie theaters. You can believe we ate a lot of popcorn that day.

We also spent many Saturdays at the radio station, where Diana helped me with selecting music for my shows and dictating album titles so that I could label them in braille. During the week Diana worked full-time as a secretary for the Hotel Papagayo.

Two of our close friends were Lou and Sandy Pardo. Sandy was from Canada and had met Lou when he was there in training at the Canadian National Institute for the Blind. Both were visually impaired. Lou worked as the director of a private local rehabilitation center for the blind, supported by the Junior League of Mexico.

One day in February 1959, Lou and Sandy told us that they were expecting a baby and planned to move from their one-bedroom apartment to a two-bedroom one in the same building. Jokingly they suggested that we ought to get married and take their old apartment. The rent, they said, was very reasonable. Their apartment was in Las Lomas, just two blocks off the Reforma, a convenient location for both Diana and me to get to work and school.

Although neither of us had mentioned marriage, we had for sure both been thinking about it. That afternoon, as we rode in the taxi to Diana's house, I said: "You know, that was not a bad idea that Lou and Sandy had."

"Which one?" Diana asked a little puzzled.

"About our moving in to their old apartment when they move out in April."

"Well, my father would never let me do that unless we were married," she replied.

"Well, we could do that too," I answered.

"Get married"? she asked.

"Sure, why not? We love each other don't we"? I replied.

"Yes." She said simply.

"Well then, shall we do it?" I asked.

"Okay", she agreed. And that is how I proposed to my wife.

Of course, conceiving the idea and achieving it were two different things. First, I had to ask for her father's permission.

Simon Bolivar Lizama was a man of strong opinions, unusual intelligence and great personal pride in his family and his accomplishments. He was self-taught in English and mastered it very well, including popular slang and colloquial expressions. In addition, he was a gifted pianist who especially loved playing American jazz. Sr. Lizama was also very proud of his five children, two boys and three girls. Diana is the middle child.

When Diana was 13, her mother died of cancer and her father remarried shortly afterward. Her first stepmother, Maria, whom I met, was demanding, abrasive and resentful toward the attention Sr. Lizama showed his children. She especially exhibited this resentment toward Diana and her younger brother, Oscar.

From the beginning, fortunately for me, Diana's father liked me. He enjoyed conversing with me in English and appreciated the fact that I knew and liked a lot of the pop American jazz classics he had taught himself to play. So, when the day came for me to pop the question to him about getting his permission to marry his daughter, I felt pretty confident that he would consent.

Diana was 19 and didn't really need her father's permission to get married, from a legal standpoint. Yet, we weren't about to go against his wishes.

About a week after our conversation in the taxi, I went over to Diana's house to talk with her father. He was in a congenial mood, having just gotten off work from his job as flight control chief with Mexicana Airlines. We exchanged the usual pleasantries for a few moments. Then, I asked if I could speak with him in private.

We were left alone in the living-room. He sat facing me expectantly. I suspect he already had an idea about what I was going to say. Diana and I were together almost every day—at her house or at the radio station, going to the movies, walking in the park, eating out. Our deep love for one another was clearly evident. I began by telling him how much I cared for his daughter and that I believed she felt the same toward me.

"We want to get married and very much want your consent and blessing." I said.

"Have you thought it through moneywise?". He asked.

"Oh yes, sir." I replied. "Adding together the income from Diana's job, mine from the radio station, and my scholarship money, I think we can do just fine."

The next thing he asked was how soon we were planning to get married. The first answer I gave to this question was definitely the wrong one.

"Well", I said, "we had originally planned to wait until June, but now something has come up, and we want to do it in April."

"Oh"? he responded with obvious concern.

I realized my blunder. Oh my God! I, the great communicator, had used a terrible choice of words. What could her father be thinking other than the worst? Lucky for me he was a civilized man and waited for my explanation.

Red-faced and embarrassed over my gaffe, I hastened to tell him about the apartment which our friends Lou and Sandy would be giving up in April, and how perfect it would be for us.

Definitely relieved, he said "I'll go and speak now with Diana. Wait for us here please."

A short time later, they both returned to the living-room and Sr. Lizama gave us his blessing. "I hope you will both be very happy together." He said.

Then he called his wife to bring glasses and whiskey and he and I drank a toast.

Diana told me later that her father had asked her if she had considered that one of the reasons why I might want to marry her might be to obtain my working papers. It was very difficult for a foreigner to obtain permission to work in Mexico. One either had to enter the country as an investor in business, be brought in as an expert by an established firm, or marry a Mexican citizen. Diana was able to reassure him that this was not my motive. She also confirmed my story about the apartment.

Our next hurdle was getting done all the necessary paperwork, with the civil authorities and with the catholic archdiocese. No small task. There were forms to fill out, lots of forms. Blood tests. Diana had to face an interview with her local parish priest about the suitability of this American for her husband.

For my part, I had to request my baptismal records from Chicago. There were multiple visits to government offices. Arrangements for the Mass, the flowers, the wedding dress, the rings. We planned to get it all done in 6 weeks. I'm not sure how, but amazingly we did.

It was a small but beautiful wedding at Diana's local parish, El Divino Redentor, in the Colonia Roma. Her sisters were her bridesmaids and Lou Pardo was my best man. But this best man almost made me miss my wedding.

The morning of my wedding I had to work at the radio station. Nothing unusual about that. Radio people frequently have to worked on Christmas, New Year's Eve and their birthdays. So, I saw no problem with this. My shift was over at 10:30 a.m., and the wedding was set for 11. A quick taxi ride, and I'd be there in 10 minutes.

Already dressed in my dark blue suit, white shirt, and tie, I was ready to make my appearance. But Lou had other ideas.

"Let's go get a cup of coffee down the street," he urged.

"I don't think we have time," I protested.

"Sure we do," he cajoled.

Against my better judgment I let him whisk me down the street and around the corner to a Chinese cafe. I sat nervously as he leisurely sipped his coffee, smoked a cigarette, and chattered away. Looking at my watch I saw it was eleven o'clock.

"Your watch is fast," Lou admonished. "It's only ten minutes to."

I knew he was wrong and got up to leave. Grudgingly, he followed. Outside I walked briskly, almost ran, back to the church. As we entered the vestibule, one of Diana's brothers told me the priest was on the verge of canceling the wedding, and Diana was on the verge of tears. I felt awful as I took my place beside the altar and waited for my beloved to come down the aisle. I wanted to wrap her in a warm embrace right then and there, and tell her how sorry I was to have caused her such anxiety on this day of all days. But I had to wait. There were rituals to be performed, vows to be spoken, and pictures to be taken. Later, when we were alone, I would tell her.

Lou had intended it as a harmless macho prank. He didn't realize, I'm sure, just how much anguish it caused both Diana and me. I never spoke of it with him but, because of it, I lost a little of my trust in him as a friend.

CHAPTER 13—NO FLOWERS FOR LARRY

Returning home one afternoon from school around two o'clock, I was looking forward to a good meal and a couple of hours rest before having to be at the radio station. It was early fall. The sun was still warmly bathing the sidewalk as I stepped from the bus and strolled east along Vosgos street to the corner. Stopping at the intersection, I listened carefully for the sound of on-coming traffic. Hearing none, I leisurely crossed south to the panaderia (bakery) and then turned east again to cross over Montes Urales and continue down Vosgos to our apartment.

I stepped from the curb and had taken only two or three paces when I heard the rumbling sound of an approaching truck. Hesitating, I thought it best to let it pass before continuing my progress. I stopped where I was. Since there were no other vehicles approaching from any direction, I felt certain that the driver of the truck would easily view my tall figure and give me a wide birth. In hindsight, I know that I should have retreated to the curb and waited there safely until he had passed.

From the sound I could tell that the truck was approaching at a slow rate of speed. I stood about four feet from the curb patiently waiting, cane in one hand and briefcase in the other. I listened attentively. He's almost to the corner. Now he's crossing the intersection. Mmh, I don't hear him. Bump! Just before the impact I could no longer hear his motor. Two seconds later I'm sitting on my butt in the middle of the street, stunned and surprised. How is it possible he hadn't seen me?

From the shoe repair shop across the street neighbors came running to my aid. "Are you okay?" they asked with genuine concern.

"I think so." I replied, not quite sure.

With their help, I scrambled to my feet and staggered across the street. My left hip felt like someone had hit it with a hammer. Feeling dazed, I decided that instead of trying to walk the rest of the way home right away, it would be better to sit down for a moment at the entrance to the shoe repair shop and collect myself. As I did, I could feel the blood leaving my face and neighbors' voices becoming distant. Sensing that I was going into shock and about to faint, I chose to lie down right there on the cement floor of the shop. This, of course, created increased anxiety for the shop owner and the others present. I knew it was better than falling on my face.

"Honey, are you alright?" It was Diana. One of the neighbors had run to our house and told her of the accident. Since she is an everlasting pessimist, on hearing the news, she thought the worst. Of course, the sight of me stretched out there on the floor of the shoe repair shop only added to her fears.

"I'm fine," I told her, "just feeling a little faint."

"Can you walk?" she asked.

"I think so." I replied and struggled to my feet.

Still feeling rather woozy, my left hip now really throbbing, I put an arm around her shoulders and started walking home. In that moment, a neighbor rushed up and said, "The police are here and want to know if you want to press charges or make a statement."

"No," I responded. "It wasn't his fault. It was mine."

Diana and I slowly walked the short block to our building. We climbed the two flights of stairs to our apartment. Once inside, I slumped down on the sofa and asked her to pour me a drink. She brought me my favorite, a tall glass of Ron Castillo rum with Agua de Tehuacan, mineral water. I sipped it slowly. Taking stock of my injury, I realized how fortunate I was to have just a badly bruised hip and bruised ego.

Diana asked for the details of what had happened. I sheepishly described my foolish action of stepping off the curb and standing there expecting the truck driver to see me and go around me. She responded by both scolding and consoling me.

I was supposed to work at the radio station that evening and do my two-hour show. I certainly didn't feel up to it though. I asked Diana to call and explain what had happened and have someone else cover my shift for that evening. With a little rest and some Bengay, I expected to be okay by the next day.

The next morning I awoke feeling pretty good, until I tried to get out of bed. My left leg buckled as the pain in my hip reminded me of my unpleasant encounter the day before. Diana heard me groan and insisted on taking a look.

"The bruise is about two and a half inches in diameter and a startling shade of purple." she observed. "It looks like a tattoo." She quipped.

"Well, it's not." I replied a little gruffly.

She repented. "Do you want to go see the doctor?"

"No," I responded stoically. "A couple of aspirin and some warm compresses and I'll be all right."

At about ten o'clock, I was sitting fully dressed on the sofa watching a soap opera on TV. There was a knock at the door. Diana went to answer. It was Cecilia, one of the secretaries from the radio station.

"I came to see how you were doing," she began. "I see you're doing okay." She continued looking at me lounging in front of the TV set and not seeing any bandages.

"I'm much better," I replied, not picking up on her subtle sarcasm. "The bruises are where you can't see them." I added.

"Oh sure," she replied dubiously. "When will you be coming back to work?"

"I hope to make it for my shift tonight." I responded.

"Did you see the doctor?" she inquired.

"He's too macho for that." Diana put in.

"Well, we were all quite worried. Glad you're doing okay." She hesitated and then added "I guess I'd better be going. See you later."

"Right, thanks for coming," I replied.

And with that she turned quickly and left.

"What a strange thing!" Diana remarked.

"What was strange?" I asked puzzled.

"She had a bouquet of flowers in her left hand when she came in, but as soon as she saw you, she hid them behind her back. I thought she was going to give them to you but then, for some reason, changed her mind."

"Well, I guess I didn't deserve them. I didn't look injured enough. She must have thought it was all an act, just a way to get out of work."

CHAPTER 14 – CHANGES:
BABIES, BILLS AND BREAKING THE HABIT

Danny, our first child, was born in March of 1960. We were very proud parents but also very nervous and inexperienced. Once when Danny was about three months old, Diana left him on our bed while she went to the next room to get a clean diaper and the baby powder. When she returned she couldn't find him. She called to me frantically. "Honey, come here. Someone has kidnapped our son."

I rushed into the room. "But how?" I asked.

"I don't know." she said half sobbing. "But he was here two minutes ago and now he's not."

"He has to be." I insisted. "Nobody's come into the apartment, and we're on the second floor."

Just then we heard a muffled cry. Looking down, there next to the bed in a waste paper basket, nestled in amongst discarded tissue and his blanket was our son. He somehow had wriggled his way to the edge of the bed and slid off into the basket. We laughed with joy and relief. Quickly retrieving him, we checked him over and found he was no worse for wear.

On another occasion, we were returning home by taxi from Diana's father's house. We noticed that Danny had been very still, for a very long time. Becoming alarmed, Diana asked, "Is he all right?"

"I think so." I said somewhat uncertainly.

"Try shaking him." she urged.

I gently shook our infant son. He didn't stir. Diana placed her face next to Danny's. "I don't think he's breathing." she cried, now in a state of panic.

"Take us to the hospital on Montes Urales". I told the cab driver. "and hurry."

Our chauffeur stomped on the accelerator and the taxi shot ahead careening around the corners. I shook Danny again, anxiously trying to revive him. Suddenly he let out a loud cry of protest. We had awakened him from a deep and peaceful sleep. Embarrassed but deeply thankful to God I told the driver the emergency was over and to take us home. Being new parents, we were discovering, was a scary business.

It got easier though with our second child Luana. And, by the time Shirley, our second daughter came along, we were feeling like old pros. And, there were three more after her.

Meanwhile, major changes were happening at Radio Capital. Advertising revenues were down. The owner, Don Fidel, was persuaded that he could make a lot more money by broadcasting in Spanish during the prime time morning and evening hours rather than in English. And so, Radio Capital's English language programming was reduced from 5 hours a day, 7 days a week, to just 1-1/2 hours six days a week and moved to 10:30 at night. Luckily I was kept on as the only English speaking announcer. Two years later, Don Fidel generously extended my program from an hour and a half to two hours each night.

Because of Radio Capital's very limited music library, and no budget to buy new records, I chose a format which featured middle of the road music—Frank Sinatra, Doris Day, Eddie Fischer and the like. We had a small but loyal older audience.

The English language broadcast began with a 15-min. newscast each evening prepared and read by a Mexican journalist, Armando camacho, who also wrote a popular column for one of the Spanish daily newspapers. Mr. Camacho had a beautiful deep voice and cultured British accent. He was a really kind man, inviting Diana and me to his home on a couple of occasions for dinner.

Unfortunately, Mr. Camacho was given to drinking before the broadcast, and often arrived at the studio so inebriated that his speech was slurred almost to the point of being unintelligible. Although the sponsor of the newscast was a close friend of Mr. Camacho's, the news broadcast lasted only a few months, no doubt in part at least because of complaints from listeners.

It was during this period that I met Felipe Carrillo, a young blind man born in Merida, Yucatan and educated in the U.S. Felipe spoke very good English. He also loved American jazz and had an outstanding record collection of top name jazz artists. Since Radio Capital's record library was totally void of this genre of music, and believing it would add some variety to my nightly broadcast, I persuaded the station management to let me bring Felipe in once a week on Saturday evenings as a guest deejay to play some of his jazz records. It was fun working together, and our audience enjoyed the innovation.

Then, we got the idea of purchasing a microphone and broadcasting my show from his apartment via telephone line. It worked great. I'd announce the music, and the console operator back at Radio Capital would play the records. It was so much nicer to be broadcasting from a comfortable easy chair with a glass of kahlua or creme de mint over ice in hand.

Yes, I admit my commitment to program excellence was not very high at this point in my career. No one at Radio Capital, certainly not the owner, seemed to care how I did my show or even if I did my show.

I learned how to pretape my programs so that I could take off from time to time. First, I'd select the records to be played

103

and type up a list for the console operator. Then I'd record my introductions to the music on tape, along with my ad lib comments, promos and commercials. I'd give the tape, the list and the stack of records to the on-duty console operator and go home early. Most of the operators knew just enough English to follow along with my tape and usually would play the records in the right sequence.

Felipe taught me how to play cribbage, and we spent many an hour at my place or his honing our skills and sharing a glass or two or three of our favorite licores. Felipe also had incredible abilities as an auto mechanic. He did most of the maintenance on his Mom's Mercedes-Benz. He could tell the make and model of a car just from the sound of its motor. I was amazed. Felipe later moved to Acapulco and established a very successful rug-cleaning business.

Johnny Hannes, a young high school student from the American High School, began visiting the station on Friday evenings. He asked if he could bring some of his own record to play on the air. I agreed. He brought some of the popular hits of the day by artists like the Smothers Bros. and Kingston Trio. He offered to operate the turntables in the control room. The station's console operator was happy to let someone else do his job. Listeners began calling in and requesting songs, and we complied. Gradually we began drawing a more youthful audience. I didn't know it then but this was the beginning of my metamorphosis from easy listening musical host to Top 40 deejay.

Johnny graduated from high school and moved with his family to South Texas. His voice deepened. He began working in radio first as an announcer/deejay in Weslaco and then later in the prime market of Houston. He also started up a sound recording studio, Jay West Productions, and produced commercials for many ad agencies and sponsors. We stayed in touch throughout my broadcasting career, sharing ideas, collaborating on productions and swapping stories. His older brother Gary also worked many years in Mexico as an English language announcer for a rival radio station.

Because of the marginal salary I was earning at Radio Capital, I needed to find other sources of income to support my growing family. I became an English language instructor with a small private academy, called Instituto Mexicano, teaching classes there four nights a week. The director of the academy, Professor Jose Cervantes, took a liking to me and invited me to help in the creation and recording of two albums of English instructional courses. I enjoyed doing this work. It was fascinating to discover how English colloquial expressions and idioms were put together and how best to convey their meaning in Spanish. Just by adding different prepositions to a common verb could change its meaning totally. For example "bring". How different the meaning if we say: "bring up", "bring on", "bring out", "bring down", "bring about", "bring upon", or "bring in". Each usage has its own special purpose and meaning.

While working at the Instituto Mexicano I made an important decision about my personal health. I'd been a smoker for 17 years. I began smoking in high school at age 15 and was now 32. I smoked both cigarettes and a pipe. I liked best the unfiltered dark tobacco cigarettes of Mexico called Soberbios, and my favorite pipe tobacco from the States was Vermont Maple.

One spring day in 1965 while talking with Professor Cervantes after class, the subject of smoking came up. "You know", I said, "I would really like to quit smoking."

"I would too." he replied.

"So why don't we do it, together"? I suggested.

"Okay." he agreed. We shook hands and that was it.

I don't know if Professor Cervantes stuck with it. But, from that day forward I have never smoked again.

There was a lot of social pressure at first. Friends and colleagues teased and mocked my decision, occasionally punctuating their opinions by blowing smoke in my face. During those first months after quitting, I found myself standing in front of a class of students with my right hand raised, the index and middle fingers pointed skyward, about 3/8 of an inch apart, holding an imaginary cigarette. When I would realize what I was doing, I'd become embarrassed and quickly take out my keys or pick up a pen or pencil.

It's true, there were some temptations early on. I remember dreaming about smoking. I'd wake up feeling guilty and then be greatly relieved when I realized it was just a dream. There were also those times when, standing outside waiting for a friend or a taxi, I'd suddenly catch a whiff of a freshly lit cigarette or pipe. Inhaling deeply, I'd secretly and vicariously enjoy the nostalgic aroma and moment. It was especially hard to resist the temptation when at a party or when sipping a cup of delicious coffee at the end of a satisfying dinner.

But those longings soon faded. Instead, I discovered that close proximity to someone smoking caused me genuine discomfort, and the smell of smoke became unpleasant. I also found that there were a lot of pluses to not smoking—no more burn holes in my pants and shirts from falling hot ashes; no more nicotine-stained fingers or teeth; and no more smokers morning headaches and nausea.

The fact that Radio Capital had opted to retreat from the English speaking market opened up opportunities for other radio stations to launch English language programming. And several did. At one point there were four Mexico City radio stations broadcasting some hours of English language programming. This eventually led to my being able to work more hours in radio and to do voice-over commercials for these stations.

One of these was XEVIP, owned and operated by Radio Programas de Mexico. They launched a 24-hour all English format in 1965 and became a CBS affiliate the following year. When the international Olympics came to Mexico in 1968, VIP Radio was prepared to offer full coverage, but needed an expanded crew of professional English-speaking announcers. And so, I was invited to be one of the anchors for 4 hours each day throughout the cycle of events. It was great fun.

CHAPTER 15 — "PIPO THE HIPPO"
AND THE FOURTH OF JULY

It was in October of 1963 when I began selling advertising space part-time for the American Society of Mexico's monthly English language magazine. The publication circulated among some 20,000 Americans residing in Mexico City. Articles focused mainly on local events happening within the American community.

I made a couple of good sales and impressed Editor Joe Martinez. Then Mr. Martinez decided to retire and move to the States. The new editor, Ruth Robertson, told the organization's officers that she knew nothing about advertising and didn't want that responsibility.

A lucky break for me. I was given the opportunity to become the full-time Advertising Manager. Although it paid strictly commission, there were a lot of good accounts. Many of the advertisers had been with the magazine for years, and renewing their contracts was quite easy.

I enjoyed the challenge of sales and the opportunity it gave me to meet many top executives with American firms doing business in Mexico.

Early on, Diana drove me to a lot of my sales appointments. Sometimes those appointments would take over an hour as I waited to see the owner or advertising manager and finally got to make my presentation. Diana would bring along her knitting and make mufflers and sweaters for the kids and me. Thinking back on it now, she had extraordinary patience. I still have many handsome sweaters, vests and mufflers knitted by my loving wife during those long hours of patiently waiting for me to complete a sales call.

I made it a point not to tell a new customer over the phone that I was blind. I liked to surprise them. I would mark up my sample copy of our magazine in braille and amaze the customer by easily flipping to the different ad sizes and describing them to him. For the small customers who didn't have ad agencies, I designed their ads and wrote their copy. It was a wonderful job, very satisfying, and it provided a good income for our growing family.

Within the American community in Mexico, the highlight event of the year was the annual Fourth of July celebration at the American School grounds. It was, in part, a fund-raising event for many organizations like the Boy Scouts, the ABC Hospital, the Junior League, United Community Fund, and others.

Several thousand people would gather on the Saturday closest to July 4 for an all-day celebration of U.S. Independence Day. There were games for the kids—three-legged races, sack races, egg toss competitions and more. There were also games of chance like roulette, ring toss and darts. My daughter Luana's favorite was the fish pond with its guaranteed prizes of toothbrushes, tubes of toothpaste or bars of soap, for every kid who participated.

There was food of all sorts—hot dogs, hamburgers, ice cream cones, cotton candy, tacos, popcorn, pizza and barbecue. There was a parade and lots of music.

I regularly covered the event for Radio Capital, tape recording the sounds of the celebration and capturing the enthusiastic and excited comments from those attending. After taping a couple of hours of the celebration I would go back to the studio and edit the tape for broadcast that evening.

Many U.S. companies participated in the event to promote their image and their products. There were lots of freebees— giveaways which the children loved.

I believe it was for the 1971 celebration that Arnold Bilgore, another English language announcer working for a competitive radio station, proposed that we commercialize the event and sell exposition booths to interested firms.

The sponsoring organization of the annual 4th of July picnic was the American Society of Mexico. The organization's officers approved the plan, and Arnold and I formed a business alliance. We contracted with a company to build the booths for the one-day event. Then we marketed the idea to the corporate community. It was a marvelous commercial success. The American Society received added income for its operation, and Arnold and I earned a nice commission.

The following year we repeated the enterprise. This time though, instead of having individual booths constructed for the participating companies, we hired a circus and had them set up their Big Top right there on the school grounds. They brought clowns and jugglers and aerial acts and a hippopotamus. He was the highlight of the show. Many young children, including our three-year-old son Alan, got to ride on "Pipo the Hipo".

The exhibitors got to set up their displays under the Big Top. It was a terrific show and a terrific success, despite the fact that there were down-pours throughout the day. But that was typical for July, one of the rainiest months in Mexico.

CHAPTER 16—MISTAKEN IDENTITY

As I mentioned in an earlier chapter, most of the years that I worked as a deejay at Radio Capital, I worked the late evening shift, completing my tour at 12:30 a.m. Buses had stopped running by that hour and so, unless I got a ride from someone at the station, I would take a cab home.

Flagging down a taxi in Mexico City back then was pretty simple. All you needed to do was stand at the curb with your hand extended, and if the cab coming by was empty and interested in a fare, it would stop and you got in.

On one occasion, I had been waiting only a short time when a car stopped in front of me. "You're going to Vosgos Street in Las Lomas, right?" a voice asked in Spanish.

"Yes, that's right," I responded, reaching for the door handle.

"Get in." the driver said.

I was pleased to find a cab driver who apparently had taken me home before and knew where I lived. I got in and settled back to enjoy the short, fifteen minute ride west along the Paseo de La Reforma, past the lovely fountain and statue of Diana the Huntress, along the lush green fringes of Chapultepec Park with it historic castle and modern museum, past the monstrous National Auditorium and on out into the western suburbs of Mexico City, Las Lomas, where we lived.

Slowly I became aware that something was not quite right. What was it? I asked myself. Something was different. And then it came to me. The meter of the taxi was not clicking off the distance every tenth of a kilometer as it normally would. I wondered why the driver was not using his meter. Did he remember what it cost the last time he took me home? Or was he just planning to trust me to pay him the right fare?

The more I thought about it, the more curious I became. As we pulled into my street, I pulled out some money and asked in Spanish, "How much do I owe you, friend?"

"You don't owe me anything," he replied. "I am your neighbor and, well, I saw you standing there and thought you might like a ride home."

Stuffing my money back into my trouser pocket, I stammered some words of apology and of embarrassed appreciation.

Over the years I've had many such embarrassing moments. Sighted people expect blind people to recognize them by their voices. Some I easily can, while others are quite difficult.

On another occasion, again after finishing my late night show, I was patiently waiting for a taxi to come along the Reforma Boulevard. It was near one in the morning.

Suddenly, a car stopped at the curb. The door opened and a man called my name as he stepped on to the sidewalk. "Hello, Larry." he said in English. "Can we give you a ride somewhere?"

"Yes, thank you. That would be great." I replied, trying to remember a name that would go with the voice of this kind Samaritan.

"Be careful getting in," he said.

I stepped into the car and reached for the seat. It wasn't there. Somewhat bewildered, I extended my hand further and touched thick carpeting on the floor.

"Back here," a female voice called.

Regaining my balance, I found a place on the plush divan-like rear seat, gently guided there by a soft gloved hand. The man stepped in, closed the door and sat next to me.

"Where can we drop you, Larry?" he asked.

"Oh, uh, I live on Vosgos Street in the Lomas." I said, still trying to figure out who these friendly neighbors were. Obviously they were American and quite rich, being driven around in a chauffeured limousine. Perhaps he was the president of one of the many American companies which had major investments in Mexico. But which one?

My new day-time job as Advertising Manager with the American Society of Mexico's monthly magazine provided me with the opportunity to meet a number of American corporate executives. No doubt many of them would remember me. But, unless I could relate the person to the particular company they worked for, it was very difficult to recognize them by voice alone, especially meeting in a different setting such as this. I decided to make small talk and see if one of my companions would give me a clue as to who they were.

"Tony and I are just coming from a party," the lady was saying.

So, the man's name was Tony. I was stumped. I couldn't think of anyone I knew named Tony. "I just finished doing my program on Radio Capital," I volunteered.

"Do you get home this late every night?" she asked with concern.

"I'm afraid so." I said. "But I'm kinda used to it." I added.

"It has to be a tough job being a disc jockey, always sounding enthusiastic and cheerful," commented the man named Tony.

"It is," I confided, "but I enjoy it."

I was getting no closer to identifying my hosts. I decided to be totally honest.

"Excuse me, Tony," I said, "I seem to have forgotten which company it is that you work for. You know, there are so many

American firms here in Mexico now. It's hard to remember them all."

"Yes, of course. Well, I work for all of them really", he explained, "for all Americans, including you." He laughed.

Seeing the puzzled look on my face, he put his hand on my arm in a gesture of reassurance and said, "I'm Ambassador Freeman. We met at the Fourth of July Picnic last month."

Oh my gosh! I thought. Here I am riding home with the U.S. Ambassador to Mexico, calling him by his first name, and I didn't even know who he was.

"Mr. Ambassador, forgive me for not recognizing you." I stammered with the blood rushing to my cheeks.

"Call me Tony, please," he urged, "and don't apologize. There are a lot of people who don't recognize me." We all laughed.

A few minutes later, we pulled into my street. I thanked the ambassador and his wife for their kindness, and we said our good-nights.

I had several opportunities after that to meet Ambassador Fulton Freeman and his wife at various official and social functions. They were very gracious, and the Ambassador always insisted that I call him "Tony".

CHAPTER 17—WEATHER REPORT

One of the nightly services which we provided to our Radio Capital audience was the weather report. Weather forecast information was not generally broadcast over Mexican radio stations. Nevertheless, I wanted to make my program sound as much as possible like a stateside deejay show. So, I turned to Diana's father, who was the Flight Control Chief for Mexicana Airlines. His job at the International Airport in Mexico City gave him direct and up-to-the-minute access to the most accurate meteorological data. I asked him if his night crew could provide me with weather information for my program, and he agreed.

Over the next dozen years, until I ended my program in 1974, I regularly provided my listeners with two nightly forecasts, one at 11 p.m., and the second at 12 midnight.

The weather in Mexico City is divided into two seasons: the rainy season, which begins in late April or early May and runs to October. The other half of the year is known as the dry season and is characterized by hazy skies and blowing dust. To add some variety to the weather scene, Mexico City is affected by storms which blow in from the Gulf of Mexico called "nortes" or (northerns) or those which may sweep in from Acapulco and the Pacific.

Mexico City, although located in the subtropical zone, has a temperate climate, due to its high elevation. Temperatures are generally in the mid 70's during the day and the low 50's at night. However, I can testify to having experienced a couple of winters when the temperature dipped into the teens, and several summers when we had some days where it reached the sizzling 90's.

Because most homes and office buildings are not equipped with central heating or air conditioning, such extreme temperatures can be downright uncomfortable. To deal with the excessive cold, residents would layer on lots of extra clothes, drink lots of hot coffee, tea or tequila, light their fireplaces (if they had them), use electric heaters, electric blankets and turn on the kitchen stove.

On those occasions when it got really hot, we'd switch on our electric fans and place a pan of ice next to the fan so that the air cooled by the melting ice would be circulated around the room. We'd also drink a lot of lemonade, bottled soda and beer. These were the times when Mexico City residents like us would flee the capital on weekends to popular nearby resort areas like Cuernavaca and Cuautla, to swim and play in cool, refreshing public or private pools.

The language used by weather forecasters is a very special one. A typical forecast for Mexico City weather might sound like this:

"Scattered to partly cloudy skies tomorrow, with a possible chance of scattered light showers likely in the late afternoon or early evening. Variable light winds from the south southeast at 5 to 10 mph., occasionally gusting to 15."

What did all this double-talk really mean? Well, it meant that tomorrow maybe it would rain and maybe it wouldn't. And, if it did rain, maybe it would rain in one part of the city and not in the other. The prognosticators were very cautious and deliberately used language which allowed for a margin of error. Even with all the advanced technology, Doppler radar, satellite tracking etc., if you listen closely to the weathermen on television today you will still hear them hedging their bet by using a lot of these same kinds of qualifiers which give them an out when their forecast misses the mark.

I made it a habit to call Mexicana Airlines Flight Control Center every evening about 20 minutes before the first scheduled reading of the weather forecast. The crew was pretty faithful about having it ready for me on time. But, once in a while, if they were really busy, they'd ask me to call them back in 10 more minutes. As it got closer to 11, I'd start feeling uptight.

One night when I tried calling, I kept getting a busy signal. Eleven o'clock came and went. The line was still busy. Then it was 11:15. I still couldn't get through. Obviously, something was wrong with the phone line. When the studio clock showed 11:30, I decided it was time to become creative. I made up my own weather forecast, with predicted high and low temperatures, cloud conditions, wind direction and velocity and chances of precipitation. I used all the appropriate vague language.

When I finally was able to get through to the Flight Control Center at 11:45, and they read off the forecast to me, I was amazed. It was exactly the same as the one I had created and read on the air.

From that night forward, I worried a lot less about getting through to the experts. If the Flight Control crew was too busy to prepare the weather report for me, or if I had difficulty getting through to them over the phone by the scheduled broadcast time, I'd simply make up my own. I was accurate about 75% of the time. And that's better than a lot of today's TV star forecasters.

CHAPTER 18—FISHING IN ACAPULCO

At the intersection of our street, Vosgos with Montes Urales, there was a small shopping area which included a dry cleaners, shoe repair shop, bike repair shop, drugstore, bakery and restaurant.

There was also a neighborhood jewelry store/watch repair shop where I took my braille wristwatch for cleaning and repair. Over the course of these visits I struck up a friendship with the young shop owner Marcos and his assistant Wilfredo. They were surprised to hear that I knew how to play dominoes and invited me to join them in a game after closing the shop.

I had good luck and beat them soundly in the first round. This intrigued them even more, and they asked for a rematch. My months of apprenticeship with Raul and his mother helped me to give a good showing. As it turned out Wilfredo and I were pretty evenly matched. Marcos regularly got the worst of it.

We also played a few sessions of poker, but because these involved playing for money, I quickly let them know that this was not for me. I opposed gambling for two reasons. First, I didn't have money to lose. Diana and I lived on a very tight budget. Secondly, I knew that friendship and gambling didn't go well together.

Once a week or so, after closing the shop, Marcos, Wilfredo and I would sit around, have a few beers and play dominoes or just shoot the breeze. One night we bought a bottle of gin and drove to a popular German restaurant on south Insurgentes Avenue called El KUKU. We ordered plates of sausage, fried potatoes, sauerkraut and cans of Seven Up. When we thought no one was looking, we spiked our Seven Up with generous amounts of gin. It didn't take long for us to finish the bottle of gin and to feeling pretty drunk.

Leaving the restaurant, we drove to a small neighborhood store to purchase some beer, so we could continue our revelry. We enjoyed one bottle at the store and took another half dozen with us. Back in the car driving toward my house, we decided to have a second round of beer, only to discover that we didn't have a bottle opener.

I told the guys that I had openers at my house, but drunks can be impatient fellows. Wilfredo stopped the car, got out and attempted to open a bottle of beer by slamming the neck of the bottle against the car's bumper. Unfortunately for him, the bottle shattered and severely lacerated his hand. It bled profusely. Even in our no care, no pain state we realized that the cut was going to need more than just a couple of Band-

Aids. It was going to require stitches. So, at 1:30 in the morning we wound up driving to one of the emergency clinics of La Cruz Roja.

When asked to explain how the accident had occurred, we did so with sheepish embarrassment. This served to return us to a partial state of sobriety and effectively ended our evening of merriment.

There is a wonderfully romantic custom in Mexico in which sweethearts and husbands will hire a group of musicians to come serenade their wife or girlfriend on her birthday, anniversary or some other special occasion. The serenade is traditionally done during the very early hours of the morning beneath the window of the beloved and is called a "gallo" or rooster.

I told Marcos and Wilfredo that I wanted to bring a serenade to Diana on her birthday, but that I didn't have much money. It turned out that Wilfredo had a couple of friends who sang and played guitar, and he was sure he could persuade them to volunteer their services.

So, on the appointed evening, Marcos, Wilfredo and his friends met me after my radio show at 12:30. We all crowded into the car and drove to within a couple of blocks of my apartment. To be sure it would go well, we decided to practice a couple of Diana's and my favorite love songs.

While we were rehearsing, a policeman came along and, certain we were imbibing, asked us to step out of the car. He was ready to take us in and/or levy us with a fine. This time, fortunately, none of us had had anything to drink, and we were able to persuade him of our good intentions.

Our spirits somewhat dampened, we drove into my street, got out and stood underneath the second story bedroom window. We sang our hearts out for about 20 minutes. By then, everyone in the apartment building was hanging out of their window to see who was doing the serenading and for whom. It was great fun, and Diana really enjoyed it.

After a couple of years Marcos decided that entrepeneurship was not for him and sold his shop. With some of the earnings he bought a 3-year-old Fiat. To celebrate the sale of his business, he suggested that the three of us drive to Acapulco for a weekend of fishing. Diana generously agreed to let me go. Marcos and Wilfredo took turns driving, and the three of us took turns sleeping in the very small back seat. This was especially challenging for my 6 ft. 4 in. frame. I had to fold myself up like a card table in order to fit in the tiny space.

We arrived in Acapulco early in the morning. After driving around for half an hour and making several unsuccessful tries, we finally found a low-budget, no-frills place where we could stay. Now we were ready for a walk along the marina and a brunch of fried fish to be washed down with a couple of "cocofish" (a local drink made with coconut milk and gin, served ice cold in a half coconut shell).

The day was beautiful and the bay calm, perfect for fishing. I had only been fishing twice before in my life. Once when I was about 15, my friend Jack and his father asked me to go fishing with them at a small lake in northern Illinois. Jack was an experienced fisherman and regularly went along with his dad. Even though Jack was also blind, he could take apart and put back together any rod and reel that was on the market. In fact, he boasted about how much extra pocket money he made by cleaning reels for adult friends of his dad. To hear him tell it, every time they went fishing, they came back with a bunch of fish. But not the time I went with him. All I caught was a cold and a bad sunburn.

The second time I went fishing was with Sam, a man who was renting a room at our house on Lawndale. He was a darn good cook and was in charge of an industrial cafeteria for a company on the near northside of Chicago. We became good friends. He even got me a job at his place for one week as a dishwasher during the summer.

Sam was in the process of getting a divorce and wanted to get away for a few days. He suggested that we drive up to Wisconsin and rent a cabin near a lake. It sounded great to me.

I was out of school for the summer and had no other vacation plans.

It was a lovely little spot. Lots of pine trees. The lake at the edge of which our cozy little cabin sat was about 3/4 miles wide and reportedly full of fish. Sam had borrowed a small outboard motor from a friend, and we were able to rent a boat at the peer. Bright and early the next morning, we loaded our fishing rods, bait and beer into the boat and off we chugged to the middle of the lake. The first hour passed quite uneventfully. No fish. Not even a tiny bite. But the beer was cold and the breeze refreshing. Halfway into the second hour the breeze became a strong wind. As is often the case on those northern Wisconsin lakes, the waters suddenly became very choppy. We decided it would be prudent to head for shore and try our luck the following day.

Sam hit the switch of the outboard motor, but all it did was sputter and die. He tried several more times, with the same result. By now, the wind had picked up considerably, and it began to rain. Waves were breaking over the side of the boat, and we were taking on water.

Sam grabbed the oars and began rowing, While I bailed water as fast as I could. We were making very little headway. We had no life jackets aboard, and neither of us could swim worth a darn. I asked myself how could we have allowed ourselves to get into this mess.

Then, providentially, Sam saw a speedboat heading toward the peer, about 200 yards off our port. We yelled and waved and fortunately caught their attention. Turning their boat, they drew along side of us. We explained that our motor had died, and that we were trying to get back to shore. They threw us a rope. Sam secured it to the bow of our small craft, and our good neighbors towed us to safety.

That afternoon Sam got a message from his lawyer that he needed to be back in Chicago the next day for a hearing before the judge. That ended our fishing expedition.

It was now six years later, and I was in Acapulco. And, of course, if you visit Acapulco, you've got to go fishing in the bay. Inquiring at the marina, we found a young man with a small boat willing and ready to take us out. It was a rowboat, but the sea was so calm, and this local fisherman, we were sure, was an expert oarsman and knew the ocean well.

We set sail with great optimism. The tide was moving out, so in no time at all we were about a quarter mile off shore. Suddenly, a dark black cloud loomed on the horizon. Our boat captain/guide told us there was a small squall developing, and perhaps we'd have to cut our fishing trip short. What a disappointment. As we drifted along pondering what to do, the soft ocean breeze changed into a blustery wind which began moving us further away from shore. We told the boatman to head for the marina, which he did. The tide was against us. The waves were getting higher and stronger. Oh my God, I thought. It's happening to me again, except this time there was no friendly speedboat nearby to tow us back to shore. Right then, I vowed that if I somehow survived this foolish adventure, I would never go fishing again. I thought about Diana and my two small children. What would become of them?

Slowly our small craft moved closer to land. The boatman strained against the oars. When we were about a hundred yards from shore, Wilfredo announced that he was going to swim the rest of the way. For Marcos and I this was not an option, since neither of us was much of a swimmer. At first, we felt betrayed by Wilfredo leaving us there. But actually, his departure proved an asset. The boat, now being much lighter, made it easier for our oarsman to propel us toward safety. After another few agonizing moments, we reached shore and were able to climb shakily out of the boat and stand on terra firma.

Wilfredo greeted us smiling, with a beer in his hand. "What took you guys so long?" he chided.

CHAPTER 19 — IF MOURN WE MUST

During the first seven years that I worked at Radio Capital XEL, I worked under a despotic, penny-pinching patriarch and self-made businessman known as Don Fidel.

Fidel Hernandez made his first fortune in the apparel industry selling work clothes and uniforms. He got into radio in the thirties and used the commercial voice of his radio station extensively to hawk his own wares. He epitomized the capitalistic philosophy: Profits are greatest if you can keep expenses down. He accomplished this by paying his employees the barest minimum, buying or replacing equipment only when it was absolutely necessary, and playing and replaying records until the surface scratch was as loud as the music itself.

Don Fidel did not believe in frills where his employees were concerned. There were no fringe benefits. No paid sick leave. No medical insurance. There was no soap or paper towels in the bathroom, not even a roll of toilet paper. We were forced to rough it, having to make due with the daily newspaper or old music sheets. I often wondered what daily headlines I may have carried around on my backside.

Don Fidel was a great lover of the grape. On certain special occasions, like the station's anniversary and at Christmas and New year's, he invited his employee family to imbibe with him. There was food and alcohol aplenty. Even those who were manning the microphones and turn tables joined in the merriment and in the refreshments. It made for some interesting program innovations.

The celebrating usually got under way around one in the afternoon and, for many, lasted well into the night. Knowing the condition they were going to be in by early evening, the on-duty announcers tape recorded their programs the night before and replayed them while sitting sipping their rum or brandy highballs behind a microphone which they were careful not to turn on.

The console operators or engineers, as they preferred to be called, were expected to play the tapes in the proper sequence. Since they were just as eager to celebrate as everyone else, playing the tapes in the right order, after six or seven Cuba libres, often became quite a challenge. It was not uncommon, on these occasions, that our listeners might experience a bit of confusion on hearing their favorite DJ telling them it was a quarter till midnight, when outside the sun was just beginning to set.

Taping and replaying programs was a common practice at Radio Capital for those announcers assigned to weekend and late night shifts. It was one of the ways in which the employees tried to cheat "El Patron," Don Fidel.

Never did I hear anyone say anything critical to Don Fidel to his face, nor did they ever say anything complimentary about him behind his back. In fact, rarely did anyone at the station ever say anything complimentary about anyone else, unless it was because they needed to ask a favor.

At Radio Capital, we worked in a world of habitual hypocrisy filled with repressed resentments and stifled hopes. For most, there appeared to be no way out. Their mediocre careers had shattered their dreams and eroded their desires. The blame for it all fell on either their family, their bad luck, or Don Fidel.

Certainly he did little to provide encouragement or incentive. Rewards and praise were rare items indeed. I remember one rare example of his unusual generosity. For our wedding present, Don Fidel gave Diana and me a case of beer. He also allowed me, about a month later to take off one day to belatedly celebrate our honeymoon. Diana had been stricken with severe bronchitis the day after our wedding, and so our honeymoon had been delayed.

We were invited by Lou and Sandy for a 3-day weekend to Lou's aunt home in CuernaVaca. This is a charming and beautiful resort town located in a flower filled valley some 60 miles southwest of Mexico City. We swam and played in the sun. Being of fare skin, however, I became severely sunburned, to the point of running a high fever all the next day. As a consequence, we returned to Mexico City a day later than planned.

When I showed up at work the following morning and gave my explanation to Don Fidel, he responded with sarcasm and doubted my truthfulness. I felt deeply hurt by this, but it was not the only time that my integrity was challenged by him.

One year, a few days before Christmas, I became very ill. I had a high fever and was hallucinating. Becoming quite worried, Diana went out to seek medical assistance. We didn't have a family doctor at the time or an automobile. Our apartment was just two blocks from a neighborhood maternity hospital. So, she went there and persuaded one of the gynecologists to come and take a look at me. He diagnosed my condition as rheumatic fever. He told her it was a mild case but still could be quite serious. I remained in bed for a week. I lost ten pounds, and on my slender frame, to even a casual observer, that would look like a lot.

Still pale and weak, I reported to work the following Monday. Instead of being greeted with expressions of concern and reassurance from Don Fidel, he said with malicious sarcasm, "Did you enjoy your week of vacation?"

I was stunned by his cruel remark. Later, I learned that this was common treatment for his employees. He used ridicule and humiliation to keep his employees in line. His authority was based on fear and mistrust, and that too was his reward.

From time to time, Don Fidel enjoyed practicing his English with me. I don't know if he ever seriously tried to learn the language. When he was feeling in a friendly, loquacious mood, he would greet me with "Ha-gwar-yu Meester Larrys?" He called everyone else by their last name without any mister or senior before it, but for some reason he chose to address me as Mr. or Senor Larrys. I'm not sure why he added the S to my name.

"Fine", I would say, "and how are you, Don Fidel?"

"Fine, tank you" he would reply, and that would be the end of our English conversation.

At first, when he began not showing up at work, the announcers and console operators suggested that Don Fidel had probably tied one on the night before. But then, when his absences became more frequent and more extended, speculation arose that he was ill. We never learned the exact nature of his illness. Some suggested cirrhosis of the liver or cancer. What it actually was, I don't suppose it really mattered.

When his wife began coming to the office in his place, we knew that the end was near. Finally, the word came, Don Fidel had died. There was to be a big funeral, and all the employees were expected to attend the service. I went with the Sales Manager and a group of other announcers. There was a profusion of expressions of condolence and regret, of admiration and respect.

The obligated and ritual hypocrisies of funerals has always troubled me. Are those who are there those who really care? In the case of Don Fidel, those of us who were present felt more relieved than saddened by his departure. Our concern was for the future. Who now would take over ownership of the station? Would it be his wife, who had no real knowledge or experience of running a radio station? Would the business be sold to some group of new, young entrepreneurs? If so, what would become of us and our jobs?

Following the funeral service, we all climbed back into our cars and headed for a favorite taco restaurant. If mourn we must, we must do it in the traditional Latin manner—celebrate the spirit of the dearly departed and celebrate we did. During the rest of that afternoon and evening, we toasted the memory of Don Fidel with full cups of rum, whiskey, glasses of beer, and mountains of tacos of barbecued pork and goat.

About a year after Don Fidel's death, Radio Capital XEL was sold to a consortium of investors known as Grupo ACIR. Many of the personnel, including me, were invited to remain. There were changes in the programming, new supplies of records and toilet paper in the rest-room. There were no more wild, drunken anniversary parties, console engineers asleep on the studio floors, or midnight program tape reruns.

Don Fidel's passing marked the ending of an era. Some of my more productive accomplishments with Radio Capital took place during the following eight years. I had the opportunity to influence programming innovations both in Spanish and English, and to meet and interview a host of talented artists from the United States and Mexico. Several of those interviews I will be sharing with you in chapters which follow.

CHAPTER 20—IT TAKES TOO LONG
TO SAY "IZQUIERDA"

Luis Cabero became Program Director for Radio Capital in 1963, just after Grupo ACIR took over ownership of the station and right about the time when Beatlemania began sweeping across the U.S. and Mexico. He shared this responsibility with his business partner, Homero Calles.

Together they owned two record shops which provided them with direct access to record distributors, thus assuring that Radio Capital would always have the newest hits first. This was a tremendous advantage for our station, since we were in fierce competition with half a dozen other AM stations playing the latest and newest hit records from the U.S. and Great Britain.

The two of them had very different personalities. Sr. Cabero was an extremely likeable man, quick with a smile and very good-natured. His partner, Sr. Calles, was more of an introvert. He worked hard but conveyed an air of cynicism and mistrust toward people in general.

The two always referred to each other by their last names. "I'll tell Calles to get that record for you." No Senor Calles, just the last name. They frequently addressed or referred to the announcers and console operators by their last names as well, without a Sr. in front. I, alone, had the distinction of being addressed as Mr. Johnson or Larry.

In turn, I never called Sr. Cabero by his first name, Luis, even though he was no more than a couple of years my senior. Since he was technically my boss, I felt I owed him a certain respect.

It was Sr. Cabero's idea that I do a regular weekly listener call-in request program. In order to produce a listener request program, there had to be someone available to locate and pull the records from the library as they are being requested. Sr. Cabero volunteered to do this every Friday night. He knew where the records were and could find them in an instant.

90% of the records we played were 45-rpm discs. The console operator had two turntables and cued up each record manually. Commercials, public service announcements and station jingles were recorded either on reels of tape or tape cartridges. These latter resembled the old 8-track music tape cartridges but could be played in timed segments of 10, 20, 30, or 60 seconds.

The Friday listener call-in request program attracted a large audience. Its popularity was due in large part to Sr. Cabero's commitment to obtain for us the latest hit records and feature them on my show first. He also helped arrange for and accompanied me on interviews with top name artists from the U.S. who came to perform in Mexico City. It was my privilege and pleasure to meet and interview artists such as Brenda Lee, Gladys Knight, Sammy Davis Jr., the Monkeys, Santo and Johnny Farina, the Lettermen, Gary Puckett and the Union Gap, B J Thomas, Stevie Wonder and twice with Paul Anka, among others. In later chapters I'll share some of my experiences surrounding some of those interviews.

Sr. Cabero drove a late-model Renault and, from time to time, would give me a ride home after the show. One evening, I told him about my experience driving on a freeway in Chicago with my friend Norman. I kiddingly asked if I could drive his car. "Sure, he said go ahead."

A little surprised at his quick assent, I changed places with him. His car was parked on the access road of the Paseo de La Reforma, just in front of Radio Capital. There were cars parked on both sides of the narrow street. I shifted into first and eased out into the center of the street. Moving along at about ten miles per hour, I listened attentively as Sr. Cabero called out directions:

"Derecho" (straight ahead), "a la derecha" (to the right), "a la izquierda" (to the left).

After about half a block, I stopped. "You know," I said in English, "this is not safe."

"What makes you say that", he asked with a grin.

"It takes too long to say "izquierda" (left in Spanish), I replied. We both laughed.

CHAPTER 21 — BIRTHDAY GREETINGS, DISCO RADIO

The mid 1960's were times of extraordinary upheaval and change in the music industry. Beatlemania was sweeping across the world, and across Mexico as well.

Like other forms of art, music captures and conveys the history of the times—the social changes, the moral values and the popular protests. A look back at the records and artists of the 60's reveals a preoccupation with three major themes: civil rights, sex and drugs. The themes constituted the principle avenues of expression and of protest by young Americans. The lifestyles of pop recording artists associated with drugs revealed a growing acceptance and openness by society to admit that such things did exist. Frank references to sex in music and in conversation reflected a changing, less moralistic society, a major break from the rigid codes and taboos of the past. The music represented a vital and dynamic aspect of a culture and of a time.

Down through the ages, each generation has sought to discover and to express its own identity. The mood and the message of the 60's will be long remembered through its music and its transforming social and political changes.

141

At Radio Capital, we too, were caught up in the music and the madness of the period. Under the direction of Program Director Luis Cabero, our station's musical format underwent a major transformation. Overnight we became a Top 40 station, playing the latest hits from Great Britain and the US. My two-hour nightly broadcast became the showcase for this musical idiom.

By this time, my wages had soared to the phenomenal amount of twenty-two pesos an hour, about $1.75 U.S. an hour. But people who work in radio, television, and the arts in general, do not live by bread alone, nor generally earn much bread either.

The year of 1964 was an exciting and transforming year for me. Suddenly I had an audience that was alive, an audience which responded to my invitation to call in and request songs to be played. It was an audience which seemed to care that I was there. Their energy, their enthusiasm, their interest, made me feel young and alive too.

It was such fun to be able to please listeners by playing a special request for them at that late hour of the evening. I made every effort to please them. I played their favorite records, read their names and dedications on the air and chatted with them on the phone. I felt proud. I felt appreciated. I felt that I was doing something worthwhile.

A senior from the local American High School, a girl named Tina French, came to visit me one day in the spring of '64. Tina wrote a weekly column for the English language daily newspaper called The News. She wanted to do a story about my program and about its popularity with students from the American high school. I was flattered and welcomed her visit.

Tina was a tall, slender, beautiful, brown-haired, brown-eyed 18-year-old with a great gift for writing. She was gracious and charming. She sat on the floor opposite me as we talked. She asked me questions about where I was born, where I went to school, what my likes and dislikes were. She took it all down. A few days later an article with my picture came out in the newspaper, and more young people began listening to the show and to call in.

But Tina was preparing an even bigger surprise. My 31st birthday was on August 28, 1964. Like so many other birthdays for a deejay, it was a day of work. I arrived at the radio station with Diana. We parked the car, entered the building and took the elevator to the seventh floor.

From the elevator to the entrance to the studio, there was about a thirty-five foot walk down a hallway. Entering the studio I greeted the announcer on duty. It was about five minutes to air time. He asked me to come to his side of the table and gave me a chair. I checked the telephones to be sure

143

the request lines were both working, asked about any new commercials which had been scheduled for the program, and got set to deliver my accustomed up-beat, enthusiastic opening greeting.

At precisely 10:30, I flipped the mike switch open, and was just about to shatter the air waves with my evening salutation, when one-hundred voices loud and strong shouted surprise. They immediately went into a raucous and wonderful chorus of "Happy Birthday to You"!

I was speechless. For the first time in my career as a radio announcer, I didn't know what to say. I felt tears welling up in my eyes and a huge lump in my throat. I thought I would cry. I felt truly humbled and embarrassed by so much attention from these my fans. But I also felt their love, their loyalty and their joy. It was one of the greatest thrills I've experienced in all my 22 years of broadcasting.

Those kids were great. How they managed to squeeze themselves into the nooks and crannies of the studio and not make a sound during those moments just before I went on the air was truly amazing. I guess I must have been tremendously preoccupied not to have suspected or noticed anything out of the ordinary when I came in.

There were high school boys and girls lined up and down the hallway, in the control room, the studio, and even in the bathroom. They brought a cake, with candles, which said, "Happy Birthday Larry." Standing smiling amongst them was the instigator of this surprise birthday party, Tina French. What a girl!

We had a terrific evening. I played their favorite records, and there was dancing everywhere—in the hallway, in the studio, even in the control room. We ate cake, and everyone had a terrific time.

CHAPTER 22 — A STITCH IN TIME OR
IF AT FIRST YOU DON'T SUCCEED

When not at work at the radio station or any of my other jobs, one of my favorite pastimes was playing with my children.

I used to love to play football with my son, Danny, when he was little. I would design the plays and then together we would execute them against imaginary opponents.

One afternoon we were scheming and scrimmaging on a nice tree-shaded, grassy lawn area about a block from our second-story apartment on Vosgos. Danny was perhaps six at the time. I had just completed diagramming a very deceptive end-around play. Danny hiked the football to me. I faked going straight ahead and then cut swiftly to my right, turned the corner in a flash of blinding speed, and ran headlong into an unrelenting oak tree. I fell to the ground stunned and bleeding, landing flat on my back.

Danny ran to me. He was scared. He wanted to know if he should go back home and get help. I said no.

I knew that Diana, was out shopping with our daughter, Luana, and that our maid, Lucy, would not know what to do unless told. I asked Danny instead to help me get to my feet. Slowly and somewhat unsteadily, we made our way home.

I knew that I had seriously gashed my forehead. I could feel the blood flowing, like tears running down my face. I took out my handkerchief and held it against the wound as we walked. On reaching the apartment, we were met by Lucy, who squealed with fear and concern. I went straight to the bathroom, instructing Lucy to bring ice. I knew that ice was the best thing to slow the flow of blood. I then told her to call the Cruz Roja, the emergency ambulance service.

Actually there were three ambulance services in Mexico. The Cruz Roja (Red Cross), was the largest, having one major hospital facility and several trauma centers to deal primarily with accident victims. The Cruz Verde (Green Cross), was considerably smaller but served much the same accident emergency and rescue functions. The Cruz Blanca (White Cross), had the gruesome task of retrieving all the cadavers. Local residents told stories about the Cruz Blanca being called to the scene of an accident and, on discovering the victim was still alive, would leave, stating they'd be back later when the victim was dead. I honestly don't know if that ever really happened.

In any event, Lucy did call the Cruz Roja. In about ten minutes they arrived. Two young attendants came rushing up the stairs and into our apartment carrying a portable stretcher.

"No problem. I can walk." I told them in Spanish. I removed the ice from the wound to let them take a look. By now the bleeding had all but stopped. The ice had done its job.

One of the attendants inspected the inch and a half-long gash above my left eye. "It looks quite ugly," he said. "You're going to need stitches."

I nodded. I had already examined the wound with my fingers and knew that simple home First Aid was not going to be sufficient. I told my son not to be worried (I knew he was) and to tell his mother and sister when they came home that Daddy had had a little accident and had gone to the hospital to get his head fixed up. I asked Lucy to stay by the phone in case Diana called and urged her not to alarm "la senora." My injury, I assured her, was not that serious.

I left with the two ambulance attendants. They cheerfully opened up the rear of the vehicle and directed me to climb in. There were two long, hard, wooden benches, one on either side. I supposed that that was where they laid the injured victims, or perhaps they somehow suspended the stretcher, with the person lying on it, between the two benches. Either way, it certainly didn't appear to be a very comfortable mode of travel.

After closing the door behind me, the two attendants climbed into the front seat, leaving me to suffer alone with my throbbing head. Then we began our wild ride to the Cruz Roja emergency clinic.

You would have thought it was a matter of life or death. We zigzagged our way through traffic, with siren going full blast. The repeated acceleration and breaking by the driver sent me sliding back and forth along the wooden bench, while his sharp turns around corners all but dumped me on to the floor. We arrived at the emergency clinic in short order. I was ushered into a large examining room. There were perhaps 8 or 10 examining tables, all quite plain and very alike. I was told to climb on to one of the tables and wait my turn.

After a few moments, a nurse (I guessed she was a nurse) came by and asked my name, address, and the name of my next of kin. She snapped a bracelet with an ID number on my wrist and disappeared.

Up to this point I had received no medication whatsoever, nothing for the pain nor for my injury. I wondered if more serious cases were treated any differently. (In fairness, I should state that I learned later that the Cruz Roja had a very fine record as a trauma center, especially dealing with very serious accident cases).

In the distance, I could hear the moans and groans of fellow sufferers, but somehow I felt little concern for their misery. I could only think, when will they finally get around to me?

At last, after what seemed like an eternity (It was probably more like 15 minutes), a doctor did come by with two assistants.

"What happened to you?" he asked in Spanish.

"I was playing football with my son and ran into a tree."

"You should be more careful," he commented. "Football can be a dangerous sport."

I mumbled my agreement. Why are we wasting time, I thought, discussing the relative hazards of playing football when I am lying here in pain and needing somebody to do something about it?

"We're going to have to sew this back up," he was saying as much to me as to his two assistants. Well, finally, they are going to get down to business.

I felt a gauze mask being placed over my face. The part over my left eyebrow was folded down to expose my wound which, by now, was beginning to bleed once more. I felt the sting of alcohol as it was swabbed over my open cut. I tried closing my left eye as the alcohol, now mixed with blood, came trickling down under the gauze mask. The effort drew a rebuke from the doctor.

"Don't tighten up your muscles. It will make it harder to put in the sutures." he said.

I was in no condition to argue. Besides, any muscle movement I made on that side of my face caused the pain to worsen. Vaguely I heard the doctor giving instructions to one of his assistants about how and where to put the stitches. Then, suddenly, I felt a needle piercing my skin. Thank Heavens! I thought. They are finally taking compassion on me and administering a local anesthetic. Soon, this throbbing will subside. Oh God, let it take affect quickly.

Just then, I felt another sharp stab of the needle. My Lord! What is this? It couldn't be that they are putting in the sutures without...Ouch! There was another sharp jab. They were indeed sewing my head back together without so much as even offering me an aspirin.

The doctor and one of the assistants moved away, leaving the other fellow to finish the job. Ouch! There goes #4 or was it #5? How many was it going to take? I tried thinking of something else—a plate of delicious tacos, a cold beer—but each new stab of the needle brought me painfully back to reality. I resigned myself to my situation, knowing that soon it had to be over. Although there was a slight chill in the room, I felt beads of perspiration forming on my forehead, and my breathing came heavier under the sterile gauze. I longed for the cool taste of fresh air. I reached for the mask and started to raise it.

"Don't do that! Remain still, please!" ordered the young intern. And then as if to drive home his request, he inserted the needle once more. There were six more pointed thrusts at my throbbing head, 11 in all. And then, mercifully it was over. I had survived.

I waited. The young intern left. In a few minutes he was back with the doctor who had first examined my injury. He inspected the workmanship of his assistant.

"You're going to have to do those last four over again, Enrique," he was saying. "Too far apart. And add one more for good measure."

Was I hearing right? Am I going to have to go through this all over again? This is too much. Why don't I just get up off this table and walk out of here? Then I thought, sure, I can just see myself flagging down a cab and saying to the driver, "I need a few stitches in my head. Take me to some other doctor. These guys here at the Cruz Roja are barbarians."

"The Cruz Roja? Nobody criticizes the Cruz Roja!"

Snip, snip. It was too late. He had already cut the improperly placed sutures and was deftly removing the evidence. I figured out then that I must be a masochist. I laid there patiently and suffered through the restitching of my wound. I laughed to myself as I recalled with irony the words of my grammar school teacher, Miss Baker, who used to say to us by way of encouragement: "Now if at first you don't succeed, try, try again."

Well, I guess she would be quite proud of this young intern attending me. Perhaps, I thought, St. Peter was watching and would credit this to my account.

The head doctor came over to take one last look. He pronounced me ready to leave. I all but jumped off the table. I was so happy.

Diana had been waiting for me for over half an hour. Understandably she was quite worried. She said they had not allowed her to come into the examining room to see me. She asked how I felt and how they had treated me.

"Oh I'm fine now," I answered. And then, after a pause, "but I think I'm going to give up football," I smiled, "on doctor's advice."

CHAPTER 23—THE SOUND OF
ONE HAND CLAPPING

I couldn't have done it without them—obtain my Master's degree from the Universidad de las Americas, do my job successfully at Radio Capital and handle my personal correspondence. I'm talking about sighted volunteer readers.

Of course, Diana helped with much of this. But a lot of her time was taken up with managing the house and raising our growing family. At different times during our early years of marriage, she worked as an office secretary for the El Papagayo Hotel and later as an English teacher for a private elementary school.

Soon after enrolling at Mexico City College (renamed Universidad de las Americas), I learned about an organization called the Junior League of Mexico. It was a women's organization, mostly well-to-do American wives of U.S. company executives, who got together to socialize, do fund-raising for charitable causes and support various local community projects. Someone at the college suggested that I contact the Junior League to see if they might help with volunteer readers. I did, and they responded wonderfully.

Mrs. Elizabeth Honey was one of the most faithful and longest serving of my volunteers. Mrs. Honey, was what I always called her, even though she was only 6 or 7 years my senior. She was from Canada and lived in a large two-story colonial house in Las Lomas. She had come to Mexico about ten years earlier to marry. She was now divorced and lived alone with her young daughter Pamela.

We established Tuesday afternoons as our reading time. She would meet me at the bus stop at the Petroleum Fountain monument and drive me to her house just five minutes away. We'd work for a couple of hours and then take time out for tea. I loved those tea breaks. It always meant a tasty cinnamon roll or a few cookies along with the English tea.

We read all manner of material, from principles of economics to Latin American history to Cash Box magazine's Top 100 hits. She was an excellent reader. A good reader must have a pleasant voice, clear enunciation, a good mastery of vocabulary and the ability to scan and find important information quickly.

Mrs. Honey was quite versatile. She could smoothly go from reading a book on managerial statistics to a Time magazine feature article about the Beatles without blinking an eye. At one point, we spent several afternoons with her showing me the fine craft of hand-writing. It was slow going. I frequently became frustrated with my progress. But she would not let me give up. Patiently she encouraged me to keep trying.

Years later, when I acquired an Optacon to help me read printed material on my job, Mrs. Honey's earlier tutoring served me well indeed. An Optacon is an electronic device which converts print letters into tactile images. A small camera is moved slowly with one hand across the printed line while the forefinger of the other hand rests on a metal plate which vibrates forming the shape of each letter. It is very slow reading, but it provided access for blind persons to the printed word. The Optacon now has largely been replaced by optical scanners which look at the whole page and convert it into synthetic speech or refreshable braille.

Penny Stewart was another of my volunteer readers. A friend of Mrs. Honey's, she was from England. I loved her crisp correct English accent. Penny did a lot of recording for me of my economics textbooks on tape. She was very resourceful and imaginative. To help me better understand the printed graphs and charts which appeared in the text, she painstakingly glued strands of yarn on to sheets of cardboard so that I could feel the chart being described.

Another volunteer reader of mine was Stanley McNichols. He was my friend Luis Pardo's uncle. When Lou introduced him to me, it was as Uncle Stanley, and so that's how I called him. He was a short man with a wonderful sense of humor and a great story-teller. He was also a collector of coins and inspired me for a time to take up the hobby. He gave me a number of foreign coins to get me started. Uncle Stanley lived with his aunt, Aunt Katie, in a house also in the Lomas. Though he was from England, rather than tea, Uncle Stanley preferred to take coffee at 4 o'clock in the afternoon. It was absolutely the very best coffee I've ever had.

Mrs. Billie Moody was another of my very faithful and dedicated volunteer readers. She and her husband, Russell, were American. He was one of the top executives with a U.S. tire company in Mexico. Mrs. Moody had had polio in her early adulthood and used a wheelchair to get around. On entering her home, in the Lomas, the first thing you noticed was the delicious aromas of home-made baking. She spent long hours every day baking cookies, pies, cakes and sweet rolls to fill orders from friends and neighbors. She did it more as a hobby rather than because she needed the money. My children loved for me to go over to Mrs. Moody's house, because they knew I would come back home with a box of freshly made cookies.

Mrs. Moody had been reading for me for about a year when her husband developed cancer in his arm and shoulder. The doctors recommended amputation as the only way to keep it

157

from spreading. The Moodys were both very religious and took the news amazingly well. Now they were both disabled and drawn even closer together.

It was the spring of 1966. I had returned to college the previous year to resume my graduate studies and complete my Master's. My schooling had been interrupted by the need for me to work more hours to support our growing family. Danny was born in March of 1960. Luana came along in July of 1961. And Shirley joined our family in January 1965.

Now it was May 1966 and at long last, I would be receiving my Master's degree. I invited a few friends and my volunteer readers to attend my graduation. Mrs. Honey, Penny Stewart and the Moody's came. It was a beautiful sunny day. The ceremony was held outside on a terrace overlooking one of the college's many lovely floral gardens. As I was presented with my diploma, there was loud applause. Among those applauding was Mr. Moody who, using one of his wife's hands, clapped warmly to express their pride and congratulations.

It was a wonderfully poignant moment for me. I felt tremendous joy, great relief and an overwhelming sense of gratitude. A big part of my achievements and success I owed to these marvelous people—my instructors, my wife, my volunteers, my friends, my neighbors. I could not have done it without them. I was a lucky, lucky guy.

CHAPTER 24 — ONE OF US MUST GO

For as long as I remember, during the 17 years I worked at XEL Radio Capital, Gonzalo worked there as well. For all I know he may still be there.

Gonzalo had the classic look of the indigenous peoples of Mexico. His slightness of build and boyish face, virtually void of facial hair, belied his years which were just a few less than my own. Sometimes Gonzalo performed his job as console engineer with amazing deftness and expertise. At the radio stations in mexico, announcers for the most part did only that, announce. The technical aspects of the program's production, the cueing and the playing of records, station jingles and recorded commercials were the responsibility of the Console Engineer. The announcer directed the program and Engineer through the use of hand signals, visible through a supposedly sound-proof glass window which divided the studio in two. At least that's how it was supposed to work.

With Gonzalo, however, very often the announcer would wind up being the one being directed rather than the one doing the directing. As I said earlier, Gonzalo possessed the ability, and at times the motivation, to truly excel in his chosen profession. But that motivation was not always there. More often than not, he exhibited a bored disinterest or a down-right hostile resentment toward his work. Perhaps he envied those of us who were announcers, because our pay was slightly better and because of the status it gave us.

From time to time, Gonzalo was permitted by the Program Director to do some announcing in the late evening hours or the very early morning hours on weekends. He enjoyed this role very much. His voice was mellow, and he was quite good. The proof of that was the many phone calls he received from admiring female listeners. That was, as I've said earlier, one of the favorite distractions and important fringe benefits for most of the announcers and Console Engineers. The goal was to see just how many "conquests" could be made via the telephone request line. The ladies played the game too, frequently calling at different hours of the day or night in order to win over their share of "Don Juans".

Gonzalo's job, for the most part, was not a demanding one and easily led to boredom and the need for some distraction. Two of his favorite pastimes while working were reading comic books and cremating cockroaches. Buying comic books was one of the few extravagances which he lavished upon himself. He resisted buying his own cigarettes, preferring instead to "borrow," as he put it, from anyone and everyone. These included friends, colleagues, visitors, strangers, anyone

161

who happened by with a cigarette in their hand or between their lips. He was never too embarrassed to ask. I think Gonzalo easily "borrowed" a pack a day. The comics in Spanish he liked to read were Captain Marvel, Superman, and those with satirical cartoons of lewd humor. It is sad that his obvious intelligence was never directed toward a more positive and productive activity.

The cockroaches (some people in the U.S. prefer to call them water bugs) came from the restaurant on the first floor. Gonzalo delighted in smoking them out of their hiding places in the wall, and then blocking their escape with a fiery circle of lighted strips of newspaper. He took great pleasure in watching the poor creatures hopelessly search for a way out. He then dropped more incendiary bombs into the center of the circle which spread and merged with the outer ring of fire, thus sealing the doom of those hapless roaches which did not make it back to their home-in-the-wall refuge. This pyrotechnic pastime of Gonzalo's, on a number of occasions, came very close to all but setting our studio on fire.

Looking back now I can better understand Gonzalo's lack of interest and excitement for his job and his frequent unwillingness to cooperate with me in my efforts to make my program a model of professional excellence. After all, what was in it for him? In it for me was the possibility of being heard by an account executive with an advertising agency, or a talent scout for some radio station in the US, or perhaps a rich and beautiful lonely senorita longing for some companionship. I knew that I would not be spending the rest of my days at XEL Radio Capital, that I would be moving on, returning some day to the United States.

With my program gaining popularity and attention, it became important for me, perhaps too important, to strive for perfection in the program's production and execution. I could not countenance a single second of dead air. When I threw my cue for the record to begin or the station jingle to be played, I felt it should happen right then, not four or five seconds later, after Gonzalo finished stomping out our latest studio fire.

If I announced that the next record would be the Beatles' "PS I Love You", I didn't expect to hear the Ripcords and "Hey Little Cobra". But I sometimes did. It was frustrating, at times infuriating, especially because I was so personally involved in the program.

I found out just how much this involvement can adversely effect an individual, both psychologically and physically, from an episode which occurred in 1967. I was working hard at trying to give the program a fresh new sound. I'd developed some exciting new promotional features and station jingles and was looking forward to a positive audience response. Gonzalo had been assigned as my regular nightly Console Engineer. He seemed to be doing everything in his power to sabotage my efforts. The harder I worked at trying to "tighten up" the format, the more mistakes he seemed to make.

I began to dread my 10 P.M. departure for the station each evening. I resented Gonzalo's indifferent attitude and sloppy performance. I felt trapped by a circumstance over which I had no control.

One evening, around ten minutes to ten, I noticed that one of my wrists inexplicably started itching. The next evening about the same time, both wrists began to itch and developed a strange red rash. Oddly it lasted only a few minutes and then disappeared. During the next couple of weeks, the same phenomenon happened several times more.

I didn't relate, at first, my peculiar nocturnal allergy to my reluctance to face Gonzalo at the radio station. But, in as much as the rash appeared at no other time during the day, and only on those evenings when I was scheduled to work at Radio Capital, the conclusion became obvious. I had become the victim of a psychosomatic phenomenon. The rash was the result of my own inner anguish and resentment.

I decided I couldn't allow the situation to continue. I made up my mind to speak with the Program Director, Sr. Cabero, the following day. I would demand that something be done about it, that some other console operator be assigned to my program. If not, I would quit. I certainly didn't need the measly $25.00 a week for nine hours of air-time which I was earning. As much as I loved doing the show, it wasn't worth this grief.

So, the very next day I marched into Luis Cabero's office and vented full force my pent-up emotions of hurt, anger, and resentment. He was taken aback, having had no prior knowledge that there was any trouble between Gonzalo and me. He listened with quiet patience and reassured me that everything could be worked out. He told me that he would speak with Gonzalo and get him to understand my position, become more cooperative and helpful. He promised he would do it that very afternoon. I left his office feeling relieved, vindicated, almost triumphant.

That evening, I noticed there was no itching of my wrists, no rash, no feeling of dread. Quite the contrary, I looked forward to doing the program that evening. I felt eager to have a good show. I determined that I would harbor no grudge. As long as Gonzalo was willing to work with me, I wasn't going to rub it in about the dressing down which I was sure he had received from Sr. Cabero that day.

Arriving early at the station, in a cheerful mood, I greeted Gonzalo amicably, smiled and gave him my music list. We

165

began the program. Everything went like clock work. The records which I announced were the records which he played. The commercials and station promos were played right on cue. I forgot about the weeks and months of frustration and resentment that I had felt so deeply toward Gonzalo. I felt instead a surge of compassion and forgiveness. I hoped that Sr. Cabero had not been too hard on him, but after all, he did deserve it.

The two hours passed quickly that night. On leaving, I stopped and thanked Gonzalo for a good show. He agreed it was, and said simply, "See you tomorrow." (Nos vemos manana.)

The next day I could hardly wait for 10 a.m., when I would call Sr. Cabero and thank him for his intervention. He had managed to resolve a very thorny problem and fully deserved my praise and appreciation.

Shortly after 10 I phoned the station. When he came on the line I had my little speech prepared.

"Hello, Sr. Cabero. I'm calling to tell you that everything went really well last night. I appreciate your talking with Gonzalo. It helped a lot. I hope you didn't have to get too tough with him. He did a good job," I said.

There was a pause. Then he said rather sheepishly, "Larry, I got called into an emergency meeting with the General

Manager yesterday afternoon. It lasted over three hours. I never got the chance to talk with Gonzalo." After another pause he added, "I'm glad you worked it out. You're both good talents and I'd hate to lose either one of you."

I hung up the phone in shock. How could he have done this to me? I felt a rush of anger toward Sr. Cabero for failing to do his duty. A moment later, I laughed out loud at my own embarrassment and at my own self-deception.

Yes, I learned a very important lesson that day, about myself, about our emotions, and about how we can choose to see our circumstances in either a positive or negative light. I'm convinced that it's all up to us. We make our own happiness and our own hell right here on this earth.

CHAPTER 25 – CANNED HEAT &
THE MARIA BARBARA ADVENTURE

In the mid 60's, Radio Capital's studios were moved to a new location at Insurgentes Sur 70, on the fringe of the fashionable Zona Rosa or Pink Zone.

Bill became a regular visitor to my program, especially on Friday and Saturday nights. Born in the U.S. of a Mexican father and American mother, he attended classes at Mexico City College. I'm not sure what his major was, if he had one. Bill enjoyed helping me answer the listener request line, sitting in for the console operator at the turntables and going out for a late night snack after the show. One of our favorite snacks was frozen lemon pie and coffee at a nearby restaurant called VIPs.

Bill also enjoyed going with me on interviews. When a top name American pop artist came to perform at a local club or hotel in Mexico City, we'd pack up the tape recorder and rush out right after the broadcast. Our plan was to try and catch a portion of their last show and then get an interview. A surprising number of times it worked.

Since Bill was a darn good photographer as well, he'd often bring along his camera and shoot some photos of the interview. We were fortunate at being able to meet artists like B J Thomas,

Stevie Wonder, the Lettermen, Martha Reeves, the Monkeys, and Canned Heat.

This incident happened on a Friday evening, which was our listener request night. Bill came by around midnight. After wrapping up my show at 12:30, we took off in his car to the Hotel Aristos just a few blocks from the station, where the Canned Heat, a Los Angeles jazz blues group was performing.

We arrived there in time to catch the last ten minutes of their performance, which consisted of a lot of heavy and very loud electronics. One guy operated a console which modified and amplified the group's powerfully persuasive pulsations. Their hit record of the moment was "On The Road." My feeling was that, given the size of the room, the group could have cut back the volume about 50% and would still have ensured that none of the audience would have been able to engage in small talk during their performance.

With our ears still ringing, we approached the leader of the group, a fellow in his mid 20's, with blond hair that cascaded halfway down his back. We taped a short but good interview. He told me how the group began, how happy they were to be performing in Mexico, and the fact that he had to wash and set his hair every day. His wife then joined us and told us how much she admired her husband's beautiful blond tresses. She said that she loved helping him do up his hair every day. Long

169

hair was definitely the "in" thing, thanks in large part to the trend set by the Beatles. Bill took a few pictures for our scrapbook. We thanked them for the interview and took our leave.

Standing outside in front of the hotel waiting for the parking attendant to bring the car around, I caught the unexpected fragrance of a rose. Then a voice said in English but with a strong European accent, "You like the flower?"

"Yes," I said, "very nice". and then she was gone.

"You really know how to pick 'em" said Bill.

"Who was she?" I asked.

"There were two of them," he replied, "and both knock-outs. They just got in a car with this one Mexican guy. They're waving good-bye to us."

"Is our car here yet?" I asked.

"Yeah, here it comes."

"Let's follow 'em", I suggested, "and see where they go."

"Okay, why not." he readily agreed.

So Bill and I jumped in the car and took off in hot pursuit. We caught up with them at the first light and waved hi. They waved back. The driver showed annoyance. As the light turned green, he made a quick right and put the pedal to the floor. The girls looked back at us laughing and waving.

"Can't figure it," said Bill. "That one ugly dude with those two beautiful girls."

"You wanna keep following them?" I asked.

"Yeah," he replied. "But let's use some evasive tactics. I'll go straight ahead a block and then cut right. That way, he'll think we're no longer interested."

That's what we did. After a few blocks, just as we were thinking about turning to pick up their trail, who should we meet at the corner crossing just in front of us but our mystery maidens and their jealous caballero. We received an ovation of smiles and waves from the lovely frauleins, and a profusion of frowns from Mr. Macho escort. We chose not to follow them directly, but drove ahead a block and then made a left to parallel their course. We were really enjoying the game, not so much because we cared about meeting the two girls, but more because we liked the challenge and the adventure. After traveling a few more blocks, we turned to intersect their course. Alas, they were nowhere to be seen.

"Looks like we've lost them," Bill observed. "Where could they have gone? Shall we give it up and go home?"

It had been an amusing interlude, we agreed. But maybe we could still find them. Using a bit of deductive reasoning, we concluded that most people after an evening of dancing or cabareting would stop for a late night snack or a cup of coffee.

There were not that many restaurants in the area open at that hour. We decided to check out our logic and drive by the two or three restaurants we knew of in the area, and see if we could spot the car. Our first choice was a sandwich shop called the Maria Barbara on Rio Tiber.

As we cruised past, Bill turned to me and said, "Well, guess what? There's the car." Then he added nonchalantly, "What do you say we stop in for a cup of coffee?"

"Yeah, I sure could use one," I said.

Parking quite close to the entrance, we took our tape recorder and camera with us. We felt they might provide us with an opportunity to become introduced to the lovely damsels.

Entering the restaurant, we nonchalantly took a table not too far from the trio we had been pursuing. The caballero glowered at us. The frauleins smiled and waved with surprise and delight. We acknowledged their greetings with restraint.

"What's the plan?" asked Bill?

"Well, we've come this far," I said. "I think we ought to meet the girls."

"How?" replied Bill somewhat skeptically. "That guy looks pretty mean. I don't know if we ought to tangle with him."

"Not to worry." I said. "We're just going to pay our respects."

Finishing our coffee, we ambled over to our neighbors' table. I spoke directly to the frowning caballero in Spanish.

"Buenas noches. My friend and I would like to extend to you our compliments on being accompanied by two such lovely young ladies."

"Gracias," he replied, somewhat nonplussed.

I continued: "We are with radio station XEL, and we would like your permission to interview the two senoritas."

The caballero became flustered, embarrassed and annoyed. The two frauleins, who understood everything I was saying in Spanish, gave their immediate and enthusiastic consent.

Bill and I invited ourselves to sit down. We taped a short interview with each. Bill took a couple of pictures and we asked for their phone numbers to let them know when the interview would be played on the air. We thanked the bewildered and still frowning caballero and took our leave.

Outside the restaurant, we laughed and congratulated ourselves on our cleverness. It was a most amusing and interesting experience. Their names were Rita and Ruth. They came to Mexico from Switzerland and hoped to find work and remain in the country. Their jealous escort for the evening was named Alberto. I would see them with many different escorts over the next five years. They were free and independent spirits fully aware of their physical attractiveness for the Latin male, careful not to compromise their virtue too often or for too little.

Rita and Ruth quickly became and continue to remain very dear friends. Rita is a tall blonde with the sculptured features of a "de Milo" and the poise of a queen. She was the type of girl who could stop traffic, literally. I remember a number of occasions walking with her across the busy Paseo de la Reforma around mid day. I would hear screeching tires and honking horns as drivers stopped in their tracks to admire her provocative beauty. They would lean out of their car windows and whistle, beckon, and plead for her attention. She would flash them all a smile, give a friendly wave, perhaps blow a kiss or two. She acknowledged them all. She loved the attention. I loved the attention too. I enjoyed their envy.

Rita often invited me to her apartment to attend one of her many parties and to meet and give my opinion about her latest boyfriend. Other times, she'd ask me over for dinner. (She was an excellent cook). She would talk about her problems, her hopes, her dreams and her future.

Rita was not at all bothered by my blindness. In fact, she found it amusing the way that some of her friends reacted to me. She had a great sense of humor and was not above playing little jokes on me or her friends.

One of the funniest incidents I can recall happened during one of my visits to her apartment. A Mexican girlfriend of hers, a model named Lupita, dropped by and Rita, in a moment of spontaneous mischief, introduced me as an important talent agent from New York. I decided to play along with the gag. I spoke to her friend only in English and assumed an attitude of bored indifference.

"Is your friend at all interested in going to New York?" I asked Rita. The girlfriend enthusiastically replied in Spanish that she was. "She says she is." Rita translated.

"Hmm. I will need to check her over before deciding. Is that alright with her?" I said as I took a step closer to the attractive young girl.

"Sure, go ahead." Rita encouraged. And then to her friend she explained, "Because he's blind he has to look at you with his hands."

The girl stood still as I began a slow tactile scan of her physical attributes, beginning with her hair which was long and soft, then her face, smooth and unblemished. I proceeded next to her neck, shoulders and arms. She was wearing a sun dress of light material which revealed a lot of bear skin. Then my fingertips slid lightly over her small firm breasts. Difficult though it was, I maintained an attitude of professional aloofness. As my fingers moved over her supple well-formed figure I allowed an occasional approving "Hmmm, yes."

Rita was helping the charade by telling her friend that I had excellent contacts with ad agencies both in California and New York. The hopeful model remained still. I continued my perusal of her slim waist and nicely formed buttocks. But when I began to caress her lovely shaped thighs, she balked and stepped quickly backward.

"No, no, I don't think I'm interested." she stammered. Then quickly she added "Rita, I gotta go." With that she turned and left.

No sooner was she out the door, when both Rita and I burst into uproarious laughter. "You should have seen her face." Rita observed. "She was crimson red."

"I have to admit," I replied, "I had a hard time playing my part. She has a really nice figure."

"As nice as mine?" Rita asked coyly.

"Of course not." I replied.

I became a kind of Dutch uncle to Rita. Listening to her woes, to her hopes and dreams, I offered her friendly advice from time to time, and watched with amazement the steady stream of suitors, each one more generous than the last. She received a sports car from one, a condominium from another, clothing, jewelry, trips and countless promises that were never kept. Some days she would be ecstatically happy, others deeply depressed.

She did modeling for some of the local Mexico City advertising agencies. In particular they liked to photograph her eyes which were warmly expressive and her hands which possessed the graceful movement of a bird.

Her secret hope, her real dream, was to find a husband and become a mother. She tried one marriage that did not work. Then she met an Italian from Rome. She decided that he was the one. They were married, and she moved to Italy.

Rita loved the United States, so when she was to have her first born son, she decided to have him in Houston Texas. By then, I was living in San Antonio. She called me and asked if I would visit her at the hospital, Which I did. She named her son Houston, after that city. She was very happy, very content. It's now been 25 years since I last saw Rita, and I still receive letters and Christmas cards from her every year from Rome.

Ruth is much more reserved and shy than Rita. Physically, she's a medium tall brunette with dark mysterious eyes, a sincere smile, a tenacious spirit, a very analytical mind, and a heart of gold. Ruth did not remain in Mexico as long as Rita. Perhaps it was because her practical, no-nonsense philosophy toward life was not in harmony with the impulsively unpredictable and romantic nature of the Latin lifestyle. I became for her, too, a good friend. She struggled a couple of years to earn a living as a secretary. Then, she gave it up and went back to her home in Switzerland. Her letters tell me that from time to time she is bored with the pragmatic approach to life of the Swiss realist. She still longs, I think, for a bit of excitement of living for today.

For a number of years, I received delicious boxes of authentic Swiss chocolates from Ruth or her mother. She calls, from time to time, and promises to visit me again one day soon.

These were just a couple of the many special friendships which I developed while living in Mexico—Rita and Ruth, two extraordinary people whom I might otherwise not have known had it not been for the Canned Heat and the Maria Barbara adventure.

CHAPTER 26—ORANGE JUICE, ORANGE JUICE AND STEVIE WONDER

"Are you really blind, man?" his manager asked.

Whenever a U.S. artist would come to Mexico City, I would make every effort to interview him/her for my program. On this occasion, it was Stevie Wonder who came to perform at the Hotel El Camino Real, one of the luxury hotels in Mexico City.

It was early December of 1969. Stevie's popularity was crescendoing with a string of Top Ten hits. Bill came to the station around 11:15 eager to go along and meet this big name Motown artist, who just happened also to be blind.

Stevie's last performance was to be at 1 a.m. Since my air shift ran to 12:30, and the El Camino real was just ten minutes from the studio, it would give Bill and I plenty of time to drive to the hotel, catch the show and hopefully get an interview with the artist. As soon as I signed off, Bill and I headed for the hotel. Bill had his camera in the car, and I had my portable tape recorder.

At first, we encountered some unexpected resistance. The door manager at the club didn't want to let us see the show without paying. Then I promised to mention his name on the air the next evening, when I acknowledged my appreciation to

179

the El Camino Real for allowing me to have the opportunity to meet and interview Stevie Wonder. This won him over. Oh! the vanity of human nature and oh! the power and might of the media.

We were given a table right up front. It was about ten minutes to show time. Regrettably, the room was only half filled. I asked to talk to Stevie Wonder's manager. A couple of minutes later, he came by. We introduced ourselves and explained our reason for being there. He looked at us rather suspiciously. In response to my request for an interview, he replied, "We'll see after the show."

There was nothing further to do but sit back and enjoy the performance. And what a performance it was! Stevie came on in a burst of energy. He was talent in perpetual motion from start to finish. He moved with ease from harmonica to bass to drum to accordion and back again. He sang and played with the enthusiasm and energy of someone who truly loves what he is doing. The highly rhythmic Motown sounds made us want to move in our seats, clap our hands, tap our feet. Much of the material was Stevie's own. Bill and I felt that even if we didn't get the interview, the evening had been well worth it.

An hour and a half later, when the show finally ended with the adrenaline still pumping through our veins and our hands stinging from so much applauding, we approached Stevie's manager a second time. He looked at me and surprised me with his question: "Are you really blind, man?"

"Well, yeah," I said a bit perplexed.

"Okay, then," he replied. "Maybe Stevie will want to meet you. Wait here. I'll let you know."

A few minutes later he returned. "Okay," he said, "come on."

We followed him to the dressing room where we were introduced to the star and his brother. Stevie shook my hand and said, "My manager says you're blind."

"Yeah, that's right." I said.

"Hey, that's cool man," he replied approvingly.

"Well, can I do an interview with you?" I asked.

"Yeah, okay, but not right now man, I need something to drink," he explained. "I'm just drained out."

So, the five of us, Bill and I, Stevie and his brother and manager, set out for the hotel coffee shop. The El Camino Real Hotel is a very large facility which sprawls along Mariano Escobedo Avenue for nearly a block. It stands just a short distance from the Paseo de la Reforma and in clear view of the monument to Simon Bolivar, the great liberator of South America.

The coffee shop was located at the opposite end from where we were. It was one long, straight, wide corridor. It was 2:30 a.m., and no one was around. Suddenly, I had a wild impulse.

"Hey!" I said, "Let's race." And without a moment's hesitation Stevie and his companions took off, Bill and I right after them, camera and tape recorder swinging wildly as we dashed down the corridor. I have no doubt that if we had been seen by hotel security, we would have been taken for thieves fleeing in the night. Fortunately, no one challenged our impulsive behavior.

About halfway down the corridor Bill and I decided to make our move to take the lead, but Stevie and his brother cut us off. We crashed noisily into the wall. Bill and I decided that out of concern for the equipment we were carrying, and because we wanted to show ourselves to be good hosts, we'd let them win. Puffing, huffing, and laughing, the five of us arrived at the coffee shop.

It was then I found out just how much liquid a human body can consume. Stevie told the waitress to bring him fresh orange juice in the largest glass that she could find. She came back with one of those glasses that are usually used for serving milk shakes. Stevie said, "wait, don't leave."

He lifted the glass to his lips and without stopping to take a breath, drained it. "Fill it up again," he said.

A few minutes later she returned, and the process repeated itself. Stevie raised the glass and in one giant swallow inhaled the contents. "Once more," he said, handing the waitress the empty glass.

"Wow! You were really thirsty," she marveled.

After absorbing his third giant glass of orange juice, Stevie cleared his throat, turned to me and said, "Okay, man, now we can talk."

By now, everyone was in a relaxed and jovial mood. Some of the earlier suspiciousness and apprehension on the part of his manager had disappeared. Conversation turned to music, the universal bond of understanding and communication. We talked of artists and friends and Stevie's career. We even tried a couple of times to tape the interview, but constant kibitzing from the sidelines and the late hour persuaded us to reschedule it. Since Stevie would be performing at the El Camino Real for yet another week, he invited us to come by his hotel suite the next day in the late afternoon, so that we could do a serious and extended interview without interruption.

It turned out to be a terrific interview. We spent about two and a half hours together. I came away with a lot of good material, which I divided up and used over a series of programs. Our audience loved it.

I found Stevie Wonder to be a warm, sincere, and remarkably modest human being, with a tremendous sense of humor. It is more than 30 years since I lost my race with Stevie, but I feel proud and happy that I had the chance to compete with so great a champion. That was the first and only time that I met Stevie Wonder, but it was a memorable episode in my deejay career.

INTERVIEW WITH STEVIE WONDER

LJ: Good evening ladies and gentlemen. Welcome to Radio Capital and welcome to Stevie Wonder.

SW: Hello.

LJ: When did you first become active in music?

SW: I was signed with Motown in 1960.

LJ: So you were then, what, three years old? (Chuckle)

SW: I was three months old. (chuckle) "Mommy, mommy, I got a contract."

LJ: Actually you were ten, right?

SW: Uh-huh. Ten.

LJ: Were you primarily signed as a singer or a pianist or what?

SW: My first record was—I called it "Pretty Music— but the old people called it the blues. Actually it

184

didn't make it out of Detroit. The first big record "Fingertips," was an instrumental. The only thing I did singing-wise was ad lib for about eight bars, a little bit of soul, clap your hands and harmonica.

LJ: Had you studied music before you got involved in recording or did it just come naturally to you?

SW: It's a gift from God, as you would say. I didn't have any lessons. I took a few piano lessons, but I was so ridiculous and the teacher would have to constantly tell me to don't play with my fingers flat and blah blah blah. So I had to give that up, because I didn't do it right.

LJ: Do you still play exclusively by ear or do you now play by note?

SW: I've had some music notation. I plan to go to school in January or February and major in composing and arranging at Michigan State. And there I feel that I will learn a lot of interesting things that will help me along. Eventually I would like to just write. I've done a lot of writing recently. I write the music and melody to most of my songs.

LJ: When you write, what instrument do you use to pick out the music?

SW: A lot of it is done with the clavenette which is a keyboard instrument that has a sound similar to a guitar.

LJ: There are a lot of new instruments appearing on records, the moog synthesizer, for example. What do you think of this kind of music?

SW: It's very interesting.

LJ: Do you think it has commercialability to it or is it just another experiment in something new which will pass?

SW: Well, I would certainly hope it would stay around for a while because the more instruments that are created, give music itself another color, another sound. It can stimulate your creative ability.

LJ: Have you heard any one example of this, which, to you is particularly well done?

SW: How about the "Switched on Bach" album? It was very interesting, very enlightening. I was very impressed. I'd like to have one but it costs too much money. (laughter)

LJ: Let's talk a little bit more about your music and its evolution over the years.   The first was "Fingertips" followed by...

SW: "Place In The Sun" did pretty good.   Then "Blowing In The Wind", "Up Tight", "I Was Made To Love Her" and "For Once In My Life", "Ma Cherie Amour" and now "Yester Me".

LJ: What about the evolution of the sound of Stevie Wonder over these ten years? Has there been any major difference or change of direction?

SW: Well, there's been one big change, the voice change. If you ever get the chance, play the other side of "Castles In The Sand" which was "Mother Thank You" which was actually the first record that I ever recorded anywhere. I did this with someone whispering the words before the phrase in my ear. The words were like: "If I find the end of the rainbow, If I find that big pot of gold, I'm going to give it all to you. What more could I do. If I had the lamp of Aladdin, I'd tell the genie just what to do. To take all the treasures in the whole wide world and give them all to you." About my mama. They did this song before I signed. I was nine years old.   And I started crying and the whole bit. I was very happy. I've been writing more of my melodies. And there's definitely a change. I think that by me writing I can express even better how I feel musically. A lot of the songs I might come up with the main idea, but as far as writing the body of the song I need someone else to do that.

LJ: Of your hits, which one have you liked the most?

SW: "I Was Made To Love Her."

LJ: Why?

SW: It definitely expressed the way I felt. And "Ma Cherie Amour" when it was released, it was released as a "B" side. And the "A" side didn't do anything, so they decided to flip it over. Good thing they did flip it over. I would have been starving. (chuckle)

LJ: How do you go about picking out a melody for a new song?

SW: Well, I guess it comes from all the events of the day, the week, the situation or the surroundings, the mood—and that causes me to write.

LJ: Most of your songs have been pretty much of a romantic nature, not really protest songs or social commentary songs.

SW: We're getting into that now. Because I feel like this, people will never know how I feel unless I express it musically and lyrically.

LJ: What kind of things are you going to talk about or sing about?

SW: Well, I wrote this one song called "Dad You're Not My Dad." It has to do with this guy when he was born, his father left, and then 20 years later he comes back. It's a very cold song.

LJ: Do you think the social protest song is a momentary thing?

SW: I think that now for as long as there is discontentment, there will be songs that come out like this from every country.

LJ: Any particular song which has stuck in your mind which has reflected most soulfully, if I can use that word, a social condition?

SW: I think lyrically the greatest song I've heard in a long time was the Bob Dylan song "Blowing In The Wind". It really expresses the way I feel and I guess a lot of people feel. A lot of people feel they are going through a lot of unnecessary changes some way or the other. And I think the young people are just wondering why, why does this have to continue? Why is it that for as long as I live I have to go through the changes? Why after I die my children have to go through the same changes? This is something that everyone is wondering. Why?

LJ: Steve, let's talk a little bit about the soul sound or soul in music. What is soul music?

SW: When music is done with soul, it's done with feeling. The word soul doesn't belong to just black people alone.

LJ: Does the music have to have some kind of special beat or lyric?

SW: It can have a beat, and it can have a lyric, and it cannot have soul. But if it's done by the artist, if he can put feeling into the lyric, then it's done with soul. If the music is played with feeling and you can usually tell that by the groove itself. You can tell by the togetherness of the musicians. For instance, I think the reason the Motown sound has been so successful is because of the musicians. I give great credit to a drummer who recently died, Benny Benjamin, who played on a lot of the Motown records.

LJ: Now, in all of your music is there soul?

SW: I try to sing with feeling, so I do try to sing with soul.

LJ: Well, what about the Supremes? Many people have classified the Supremes as being perhaps more commercially oriented than some of the other Motown artists.

SW: Well, I say that maybe it is more pop than say Aretha Franklin. Aretha Franklin is as soulful as you can get.

LJ: On which of the Supremes records would you say they're more pop and on which one are they more soul?

SW: Well "Baby Love" was I think more pop. Their recent "One Day We'll Be Together" has soul I feel. The song done by Frank Sinatra "It Was A Very Good Year" I think he sang with a lot of feeling.

LJ: You would call that a soul song?

SW: I wouldn't say it was a soul song. I'm just saying he sang the song with soul. Actually more attention is paid to the entertainer, to the singer, so therefore it's up to him to get the lyric across to make the music sound together. To get himself across, he must sing with feeling.

191

LJ: As a performer, as an artist which medium do you prefer to work in? Which one do you feel allows you the maximum of your expression: the recording studio where you have all the electronic facilities at your disposal, on stage where you have personal contact with your audience, or on television?

SW: I feel that all of them are a challenge in themselves. I enjoy recording and producing because it stimulates me to create other things. I can come up with an idea. On stage also I can come up with an idea with an audience to bring us closer together. I feel that I must project not just like the record but better than the record on stage, because I'm there.

LJ: But you don't have the echo chamber on stage.

SW: That's just a crutch, in a sense. You don't really need all that. You should only use those to get certain effects but not run it into the ground.

LJ: Let's talk about one of the most extraordinary happenings on the music scene in the past decade, the Beatles. What is your perception of the Beatles and what has been their influence on you and on the music industry?

SW: Well, I think they're fantastic. I guess that's the
        way I would start off. John and Paul and George,
        as far as writers, have contributed a lot. They've
        brought on many new ideas.

LJ: How would you describe their sound?

SW: Basically I think they have been influenced by the
        R.&B., you know Little Richard, Otis Redding,
        Aretha Franklin. You can definitely tell that they
        have listened to Little Richard.

LJ: Is there soul in Beatles music too?

SW: Definitely soul.   The songs "Something" and
        "Yesterday."   There is a thing there in their Abby
        Road album which reminds me of an old rhythm
        and blues type group. The Five Royals. I'm sure
        you've never heard of them before, but the
        harmony structure "She came in through the
        bathroom window by the silver spoon".   You
        listen to the harmony. The melody itself has a lot
        of the R.&B. black 50's-type feeling. So they have
        been influenced by, I'm sure, many black artists,
        plus their own talent and ability to get across a
        lyric and a melody.

LJ: What specific influence, if any, have they had on
        the Stevie Wonder sound?

SW: Well, I'll say include them along with Sly and the Family Stone as definitely influencing me. Musically, recently I've come up with some things not stealing from them, but how can you not help it? I think everybody steals from everyone.

LJ: Stevie, it's just about time to say farewell. We certainly have enjoyed it.

SW: Yeah, I'm getting sleepy. It's like about 9 A.M. We've been here all night. (Laughter) It's been tremendous though. Man, you're crazy.

LJ: I hope you have as much success with the remaining shows here at the El Camino Real as you've had these first nights, like the one we enjoyed last week. We want to welcome you back to Mexico real soon. Will you come back again?

SW: I would love to. Very much so. You try to make it down again to see the show. If you don't there'll be a lot of trouble. (laughter)

LJ: Goodnight to you and thanks again, Stevie Wonder.

CHAPTER 27 — HE DID IT HIS WAY

As a radio deejay, I had the pleasure of interviewing many top name artists, some of them more than once. Paul Anka came to Mexico on three occasions. I was fortunate to interview him on two of those. First in 1961 when he was still riding high in his popularity as a teen idol singing songs like, "Diana". His voice was young and fresh.

The interview, as I remember, was conducted mid the confusion and turmoil of six or seven other radio stations in Spanish, all trying to get the young artist to say a few words into their microphones. Because I was the only announcer there who spoke fluent English, he gravitated toward our microphone and gave us twice as much time as any of the other radio stations.

About six years later, he returned to Mexico for an engagement at a popular night club call the Forum on south Insurgentes Avenue. Since bill was not available I went to the Forum with one of our console engineers, Alejandro, (Alex as he liked to be known). We arrived at the Forum at about 1 a.m.

Paul Anka was about two-thirds of the way through his Performance, his final show of the evening. His style had changed considerably. No longer was he the teeny bopper idol.

195

Now he was singing with more sophistication. He didn't have the voice that he had six years earlier, but he had a stage presence, a magnetism, and an expressive delivery which captivated and held the audience. He was, to my way of thinking, a far better performer. He also had begun writing and arranging songs for other artists. In fact, one of his biggest hits of that moment was "My Way" which he specifically wrote for Frank Sinatra.

Alex and I hurried back stage after the performance, along with fifty or so other press and media people, to try to get a few words with the star. Our chances seemed rather bleak. The scene was a room full of people, bodies pressing against each other, flash bulbs popping everywhere, microphone cords like silent serpents entangling arms and legs.

One advantage of being tall is that you can be seen above the crowd. Suddenly, I heard Paul Anka's voice saying: "Hey, I know that guy, let him through." A narrow path opened up and I squeezed my way up close.

"I remember you," he said. "You interviewed me about five or six years ago in English, isn't that right?"

"Yeah I sure did and I'd like to do it again," I replied.

"Well it's too crowded right here. How about at my hotel?"

"Fine," I said.

Turning to his manager he said, "Give him a date when he can come by."

His manager suggested a date and time. I accepted, thanked him and we left. Alex was very impressed. "It doesn't always work that easily, Alex," I said.

"Can I go with you on the interview?" he asked.

"Why sure," I answered.

Two days later Luis Cabero, Alex and I arrived at the very luxurious Hotel Maria Isabel on the Paseo de la Reforma. It was then the hotel of choice for many celebrities and dignitaries. It was the same hotel where President John Kennedy and his wife stayed when they visited Mexico.

We were greeted by Paul Anka's manager who invited us to relax in the elegant sitting room and offered us refreshment, which we politely declined. We busied ourselves setting up the tape recorder and microphone. Sr. Cabero had brought along a camera in order to get a picture or two of Paul and me. That was a funny session in and of itself. Paul Anka is about five ft. six or seven, and I'm six four. Standing next to me, he looked even shorter. So, for the photo shot he asked to be given a stool to stand on in order that we might be more nearly the same height.

He was one of the easiest artists it's ever been my pleasure to interview. When I suggested telling him in advance what

197

the questions would cover he said: "No, please don't. I'm a much better interviewee if I don't know what you're going to ask."

And so, we did it his way.

INTERVIEW WITH PAUL ANKA

LJ: Good evening Paul Anka.

PA: Good evening to you and all my friends out there who I left behind five years ago. It's nice seeing you again, and to all you listeners, as I said, it's nice being back.

LJ: Actually, Paul, you've had two waves of popularity which is quite an achievement. How would you describe the new Paul Anka?

PA: Well, we're in a business of cycles. We're in a business that changes very fast, show business. I think the uniqueness of my situation is that I was the first kid pop singer of 15 years old who was writing and singing his own material and having them become hits. I lived that moment for what it was. With maturity and age obviously if you work at your craft, and if you want to stay in the business, and if you have anything, you mature into another kind of a performer, another kind of being. That's really what has happened to me. The key to it all was the fact that I was very young and I had a lot to learn. Consequently with age, I adapted myself to being a performer and being more of a diversified artist as opposed to being a teenage idol, just existing on hit records. There's a value line with Anka the artist, where the talents of the artist are recognized as opposed to quick flash-in-the-pan success which it could have gone to 14 years ago when I started.

LJ: Very definitely. But I'd like to talk about the period in between. Outside of performing, you've still maintained your presence among the world public with an occasional record here and there. But you have other activities of perhaps greater interest.

PA: Well, it's out of necessity. I think an artist, such as myself, being a writer, and that's really my first love, I love to write. It threw me into the publishing business. It threw me into being a producer and, because of my emotions in that area, I have excelled. In the past six or seven years I've been writing a lot for shows like the Johnny Carson Tonight Show, the theme is mine, music for "The Longest Day". Recently, I've been writing material for other artists.

LJ: What kind of material do you feel the urge to write?

PA: Well, I write exactly using that key word what I feel. I don't sit down and classify myself as a rock writer or ballad writer. I write the way Anka feels, and I've been writing in several bags. Every kind of different type of song that I do is just another expression of me. Just putting out the way I feel is basically how I write. As a publisher, and perhaps hidden producer, I put together things like "Put Your Head on My Shoulder" by the Lettermen, which was a hit. Yes, and now we have the new Sinatra song which is out called "My Way", and Vic Dana has redone "You Are My Destiny." My basic function is not trying to wear myself too thin. It's just to create the vehicle and give the song to someone I feel can do something with it and have a success with it.

LJ: Well Paul, as a person who has been active now in just about every area of the music business— publishing, writing, arranging, composing, performing, and recording—I'd like to get a few of your comments on the current trends in pop music. Would you like to make any comments on where you think it's going or where it's been?

PA: Well, I tell you, no one can really profess to have the answers. That's what makes it such a great business. You don't know where it's going to come from next. Those of us working creatively and those who feel we have our fingers on the pulse, we kind of know where the flow is headed. We know what the new kind of sounds will be or what the people want. You can never really know for sure. I think that today the major difference is that there is so much music. There are so many talented people in it. There is such a wide scope of different kinds of artists today where there wasn't ten years ago, when guys like myself and others were pioneering. It was a small little group of us. Today the adult major masses have accepted this music, and it just becomes more baffling to us. You've got underground. You've got country. Now we're going back to the old songs again. I think that the real trend for the moment will be back to the old strong melodies again. The Meat & Potato songs that the simple people can understand rather than sounds and lyrics that you need definitions for, pamphlets handed out with each record.

LJ: Well, let me ask you some specific questions. What do you think of "bubble gum" music?

PA: First of all, the "bubble gum," it really hasn't taken hold. Even with all the noise about it, there haven't been but five or ten of them to make the top ten. It has its market. They're saying now that "bubble gum's" on its way out, it's finished.

LJ: Yes, exactly. Was it good music?

PA: Well, I don't look at it that way anymore. I believe in free expression. Not everyone is intellectual enough to sit down and write good music, and not everyone out there is intellectual enough to sit down and accept that kind of music. I think it's beautiful that we're in a world or country or place today where we can express ourselves the best way we know how and it doesn't have to be good. I mean we'll suffer the consequences. I, as a writer, will write the best I can. "Bubble gum" music was, you know, for "bubble gum" kids, kids who dug that kind of thing. That kind of music will get the notoriety that it deserves. I am a firm believer in solid foundation and good copyrights. I think that they will last forever. They will always go on like anything that is solid and stable, whether it's government, whether it's business or whatever. I believe in copyrights.

LJ: This is why Paul Anka goes back to a lot of the old material for new releases.

PA: That's right. I think that the beauty of copyrights and songs is that they live on. I mean a record today doesn't have to be done just once and that's it. A good song will be a hit over and over and over again. I think the trend today with many songs like "Green Apples", "Honey", "Phoenix", you name them. These songs are being recorded and released over and over again because they're good songs and people want to hear good songs.

LJ: Would you like to say something about the Beatles?

PA: Well, I could say a lot about the Beatles. (Laughter) I think the main thing in identifying with them creatively there is no doubt about their talent. I think a large amount of resources and energies went into their songs and recordings.

They are very talented. They write fantastic songs. They've contributed, I can't tell you what they've contributed to the music industry. They've done a lot for it. The other side of it. Everyone is entitled to live their personal life the way they wish. It goes back to what I say: Everyone pays their dues. If they wish to expose themselves a certain way that's their business and they will pay their dues eventually. Creatively. That's the only way I look at them. I think that they are definitely people to contend with. They are talented people. And they'll be around for a long time, they and their songs.

LJ: Right, just like Paul Anka. I'd like to ask you a quick question about your native land, Canada. In particular, your analysis of Canadian artists and the Canadian music industry. Do you think there is a movement ahead or do you think they're still being smothered by the United States and Great Britain?

PA: Well, they have of course for years lived in the shadows, but I think that for the first time now you will find that Canada will give it a shot. I think that there are some talented people. I think that they're really going to try and assert themselves and you possibly will be hearing a lot from Canada in the next two or three years.

LJ: Well certainly Andy Kim has made it. Right?

PA: He became a national name in the U.S. The Guess Who before him, but Andy, I'd say, has made a bigger impression than the Guess Who did, even though it's been kind of a gradual growth of popularity.

LJ: I understand he was just selected by some poll in Canada as one of the top male artists.

PA: He's done real well. I found a group up there years ago. I released them on Atlantic. They were called Clayton Thomas and something. Anyway, he's now singing with the Blood, Sweat and Tears as the lead singer.

LJ: Are you particularly interested in producing Canadian groups or artists?

PA: Well, I'd like to see them get ahead. I'd like to get involved somehow. But the problem when you're one person, there's only so much you can do, and I just haven't got the time to be in four places at once. I'd love to do it. I think within the next year I'll probably set myself up that way so that I'll have people working with me who will do it for me who I will supervise. As I see it, when you love your work and you really feel you know how to do it, it's just rough when you haven't got the time.

LJ: Right. Well we know that you are currently here in Mexico with a tremendous show at the Forum and you'll be there all this week. How are things going?

PA: Well, the people seem very happy. I've been enjoying myself. The orchestra has been marvelous which makes the job much easier, and we've had a wonderful time with the Castro Brothers. It's a new experience because I've never really worked Mexico City this way. I hope the club makes it because I think Mexico City could use a good club like this.

LJ: They're off to a flying start and if they have artists of your caliber, there's no doubt about it. What are your plans Paul? Are you going to be doing a lot more club dates, recordings, TV, what's in the future? I know you're going to continue of course always with the writing and producing. In so far as the public is concerned, will they be seeing and hearing more of Paul Anka?

PA: Yes, we hope so. I hope in recordings, they'll be more of those around now because I'm into that. We have, I think, two chart records now since we've gotten back into it.

LJ: "Good Night My Love", which is climbing very well and what's the new one?

PA: "In The Still of the Night" just came out and in fact, I have a copy for you.

LJ: Great. And an LP on the way?

PA: LP was out two weeks ago. That's hittin' the charts next week.

LJ: What's the title of it?

PA: "Good Night My Love."

LJ: Very appropriate.

PA: And I'll be doing the Ed Sullivan and Tom Jones shows in a couple of weeks. My Copa Cabanna appearance April 17, Las Vegas in the summer, Puerto Rico, and that's really all I want to do in personal appearances. The rest of the time I want to devote to my writing and my recording.

LJ: Any plans for coming back to Mexico or is it still too premature?

207

PA: There's of course talk about it.

LJ: Good. Well we certainly want to wish you the very best of luck in all of your activities and a talent like yours is extremely valuable to the whole music industry. Whether it's writing or producing or recording, we'll be looking for the name of Paul Anka in the future for a long time to come.

PA: I thank you and as I said earlier it's gratifying after so many years to come back again and find you still at the helm of the ship here. You say, come back! Don't disappear! It's a wild feeling to know that some people hang in with you twelve or fourteen years.

LJ: If we can possibly make it, we'll get over there and catch another part of your show at the Forum. The bit we saw the other evening was tremendous.

PA: We're really cookin' now. We got a couple of days under our belt and last night I think I wound up with fifteen pair of shoes (laughter) and ladies jackets, some purses, flowers, napkins, and socks. It looked like a girl I was trying to get out of my room (laughter) Many, many years ago.

LJ: Thanks so much Paul Anka.

PA: Thank you.

LJ: Good luck to you.

PA: Bye bye you all.

There's a real gentlemen.   I truly enjoyed doing that interview and even at his five-foot six or seven, whatever it is, there's a man that stands very tall in my eyes.

CHAPTER 28 — "TAKE ONE"...
DUBBING FILMS & MAKING COMMERCIALS

By the late 1960's, in addition to XEL, Radio Capital, there were two other radio stations in Mexico City offering programming in English part-time and one, XEVIP, which broadcast full-time in English. As a consequence, there was a great demand for professional-sounding English-speaking announcers. Fortunately for me, My deejay job with Radio Capital provided me with a pretty high profile in the advertising community. This resulted in a lot of opportunities for me to do commercial voice-overs for many of the agencies in town.

I received calls two or three times a week from ad agency account managers or artistic directors requesting my services to do voice-overs for their clients. It became a lucrative and welcome supplement to my income.

I did commercials for all the major airlines which flew into and out of Mexico City — Braniff, Eastern, Western, American, Pan American, Qantas, Mexicana. (Several of these are no longer around.) I recorded commercials for the major auto and tire companies, banks, breweries, cosmetics, clothing stores, pharmaceuticals, supermarkets, and scores of others. I really enjoyed this work.

To be considered a good commercial voice-over announcer you have to develop timing, pacing and interpretation. It can be quite a challenge to read a commercial with meaning and expression and get it said in the time allotted. Usually it requires multiple "takes" (recording attempts) to get just the right phrasing the producer is looking for while, at the same time, managing to keep it within the time limit specified.

Timing is something you have to learn to feel, to know instinctively. Most commercials run 20, 30 or 60 seconds in length. Without looking at my watch, I could sense how much time had elapsed and would know, before the producer said a word, if my reading was too long or too short. I got very good at stretching or tightening my readings to fit the specified time—shaving off two seconds here, adding one second there. It was fun and challenging.

A good voice-over reading also requires good interpretation. This has to do with pacing, emphasis, voice inflection and pronunciation. During the 1930's and 1940's the standard in radio was the pair-shaped golden tones of voices like Don Wilson of the Jack Benny Show, Orson Wells, and others. In the 50's and 60's, however, styles changed. The new approach was conversational, more personal. Since I had studied under the old school of radio broadcasting, I had to work hard at changing my style and develop new skills of interpretation and versatility.

The copy or text of a commercial is equally important. Some of the commercials I did were straightforward sales pitches — forceful, enthusiastic and rapid-fire. Others were more conversational, lyrical even poetic. One of these which I greatly enjoyed doing, and which won a national advertising award for the agency, was for Qantas Airways. I was so proud and pleased with it that I have kept a copy of it on tape. Here is how the text read.

How long have you been alive?
What memorable thing have you done in your life? What marvelous places have you seen? What rare and precious memories do you have? Any? Lots? None? Do you have the time? Then give us your time, and we'll give you memories to last a lifetime. We'll show you things you've never seen. Take you to places you've only dreamed of. Open doors for you. Fill your life with experience and joy. We, Qantas. We'll take you across oceans, across continents, great distances, to fabulous Pacific islands. Just find the time. Give us your time, and we'll send you on a Qantas holiday anywhere in the whole wide world, and give you memories to last a lifetime.

212

A beautiful piece of prose, framed against a lush musical background, and I had a full 60 seconds to do it in.

Most of the time, I would get the commercial copy from the agency a day or two before the scheduled recording session. This gave me the chance to transcribe the text into braille and to practice reading the script out loud. Frequently I would tape and play back my readings until I felt I had just the right inflections and voice variations. It is a lot harder to pick up a script and read it cold. There were times though when I had to do just that. Occasionally I'd get a call from an agency saying that they needed me to cut a commercial for them within the hour. Not wanting to turn down the opportunity to earn the extra money, I'd hop in a cab and rush over to the recording studio. On arriving, the agency producer or account manager would dictate the commercial to me, and I would have just five minutes to prepare. The proof, I guess, that they turned out okay was that the agency people kept calling me back.

Right here, I have to say that an important part of my success as a commercial voice-over, I owe to Ron Fletcher, a fellow expatriot, who took me under his wing and taught me technique. He was my principle mentor and critic. He could be down-right ruthless with his criticism. He was a perfectionist. He had a keen awareness of the "new" sound

213

being used by successful voice-over announcers in New York and insisted on my learning those techniques. He helped me to improve my abilities. We worked a lot together. As the result of constant study and practice, Ron and I became the top two most sought-after English language voice-overs in Mexico City.

While most of the commercials I recorded were for radio stations in Mexico City and Guadalajara, occasionally I was asked to do some for stations along the US-Mexico border, a couple in California and even in places like Bermuda and Nassau.

In addition to commercials, I did a number of recorded narrations for audiovisual presentations for hotels, real estate developers and the Mexican Tourist Bureau. These might run 15 or 30 minutes in length.

Another demand for English voice-over work was in the dubbing of films. Most of these films were Class C monster movies made in Japan. They were marketed to drive-in theaters in the U.S.

Voice-over film dubbing work is even more time critical. The person doing the dubbing has to synchronize his/her speech with the actor on the screen. In order to do a good "sync", it helps to watch the lips of the actor. Since I didn't have the benefit of any visual cues, I had to rely entirely on my sense of timing and pacing.

A film is cut up into short ten-second loops. A loop is run a couple of times for the actors to rehearse the lines they will be dubbing. Then the director gives a signal to the recording engineer and announces "Take 1".

The actors read their lines and try to match the English words to the Japanese. The loop is played back and the director judges the "sync". Some difficult loops, where several people speak very quickly, might require 20 or more "takes" before the sync is judged acceptable.

One of the directors with whom I worked a lot early on was Stem Seeger. Stem was a mild-mannered, very intense fellow with incredible patience. He was liked by everyone and made us all feel important and comfortable. He taught me how to make pauses, give grunts and screams of the proper length. He'd read my lines for me once to demonstrate the proper pacing, then give me my cue with a gentle tap on the shoulder.

Dubbing sessions could go on for ten hours a day and for several days. If you had a major part, you could be spending a lot of time cooped up in a small studio with a bunch of people. Sometimes there were personality clashes. Stem was very adept at soothing ruffled feathers and handling the prima donnas. Thanks to him, I got very good at doing dubs and was called back repeatedly for more sessions. Sadly, Stem met an untimely death in an small plane crash while doing photo shooting over mountains in northern Mexico. He was greatly missed.

CHAPTER 29 — MEN ON THE MOON

My last eight years in Mexico, 1966-1974 were, without a doubt, the most eventful, exciting and rewarding years for me as a professional broadcaster.   During that period Radio Capital XEL became and remained the number one most popular radio station in Mexico City, playing American and British hit records.   Our nightly two hour English language program, for which I was the host six days a week from 10:30 till half past midnight, served as the showcase, introducing new records, testing new features, and offering a sense of legitimacy and expertise, which the half dozen other stations playing the same records, but having only Spanish-speaking announcers, found hard to match.

Each night I offered a different musical menu.   Monday night was the Top 30 Gold Star Survey based on Cash Box Magazines Top 100 hits for the week. I played in descending order the top 30 most popular records for that week. Tuesday night was known as the Triple Ten Trio. It featured 10 hit records from the top 30, ten up and coming chart risers which I labeled Radio Capital's Red Arrow Rising Hits, and ten golden oldies, million sellers from the past.

Wednesday night included a segment I called Juke Box Banter, during which I shared with the audience news about top favorite artists and new trends in the music business.

Thursday night I took Time Out For Comedy and played album cuts from some of the top comedy artists of the day, such as Bill Cosby, Bob Newhart, David Frost, Rowan & Martin, Alan Sherman, etc.

Friday night had our highest audience ratings and our most popular show called, "Your Friday Festival of Favorites". It was not an ordinary request program. We allowed, even encouraged our listeners to dedicate song titles to one another and I read the dedications, all of them, on the air. The program lasted two hours, but we took call-in requests and dedications only during the first hour. Since I had to write the dedications and requests in braille in order to be able to read them back on the air, I answered most of the calls myself, using two telephones. On the average each week during that first hour I handled between 130 and 140 calls from listeners and still managed to announce the records, do commercials, and read off the dedications between the records. It was hectic at times, but I loved it. With that kind of a format, you learn to talk pretty fast.

From time to time, I did have some helpers come down to the station from the American high school or the local college and I would let them answer the telephone and pass on the dedications and requests to me for reading on the air.

We also received dedications and requests by mail, and those had to be read on the air as well. The listeners enjoyed hearing their names and the names of their friends over the radio. It meant a great deal to them.

To heighten audience interest and participation, we frequently ran contests and gave away everything from bags of jellybeans, to coupons for hamburgers to record albums.

On one occasion I did a contest called "Deejay For A Night". The winner got to come and cohost the program with me one evening. He was an 8th-grader at the local American School by the name of Phil Suarez. More than 30 years later he called me from a town in Texas to reminisce about that highlight moment for him.

On Saturday night I led off with a 30 minute presentation of "The Hit Parade from the USA." This was the program where we unveiled some of the major chart changes among hit recordings for the week upcoming and played the new top three most popular records in the United States. This program also brought a high audience rating. Our audience, in fact, was loyal throughout the week, much to the chagrin of the parents of some of our younger listeners. Once in a while one of these parents would stop me in the street or supermarket and chide me about keeping their son or daughter awake past midnight listening to my program. In truth, the parents too, were real supporters of the show. Many of them, I suspect, listened to it on the sly.

When Radio Capital XEL was purchased following the death of Don Fidel Hernandez in 1963 by Grupo ACIR. They also acquired two other AM and one FM radio stations in Mexico City. This was quite common for one organization or group to have ownership of multiple radio or television stations in the same city. In addition, Grupo ACIR had full or part interest in some 10 other radio stations scattered throughout the Mexican Republic.

The Ascarraga family held controlling ownership of three of the five TV channels operated in Mexico City during the time that I was there. The Aguirre group owned and operated five of the major AM radio stations in the City. For the most part, different programming and air personalities would be used on each station in order to create their own individual identity. However, news features or special events programming might be shared.

This was the case in 1969 when our Grupo ACIR network chose to broadcast the lunar landing of Apollo 12, and I was invited to serve as one of the commentators, in Spanish, during the seven day coverage. It was an unforgettable experience. I spent several weeks doing extensive background research. I obtained valuable pre-flight data from the U.S. Embassy's Information Office.

We worked 12 hour air shifts. There were two Mexican announcers and myself. We sat together in a studio behind a sound proof glass window. My colleagues monitored and described for a Mexican National radio audience of several million, the visual pictures which they watched on television. I listened in with a set of headphones to the Armed Forces Radio Network to glean additional tidbits of information to pass on when it was my turn to make comments.

It was a thrilling moment indeed, and a proud one for me as an American, when the LM finally touched down in the Bay of Tranquility, and Neil Armstrong pronounced those 10 memorable words. Somehow, at that historic moment, the reputation, the image of America became again the image of the champion, the symbol of excellence and of success. Forgotten for a moment at least where the sputnicks and the memory of that other bay, years earlier in Cuba. An American who lives abroad learns, I think, a great deal more about his own country's politics and how we are perceived by our friends and neighbors. We also come to understand and appreciate a great deal more those things which too often we take for granted. Those men on the moon on that day awoke in me a deep sense of patriotism, a renewed faith in man's ability to do the impossible and an optimism toward my own dreams for the future.

CHAPTER 30 — THE AM REPORT

Ron Fletcher was a handsome, talented, intelligent, and thoroughly outrageous American expatriot whom I met during the mid 1960's in Mexico. He cataloged himself as an actor, did commercial voice-overs, narrations, film dubbings and worked as a part-time radio announcer for a competitive English language radio station.

Ron was then and still is an outspoken, opinionated liberal. He was pro pornography, pro nudism, pro gay rights and pro the legalized use of marijuana. He was anti-religion, anti-military, anti the boy scouts, anti any group which he considered promoted regimented conservative thinking.

He was also definitely pro sex. Ron saw every woman as a partner for sexual pleasure. He devoted much of his time to seducing every woman/girl he met, regardless of age or marital status and, in an amazing number of instances, he was successful. His approach was audaciously direct. He told me once, "You know if you stood on a corner and asked every woman who went by if they would have sex with you, sure you'd get a lot of slaps in the face, but you'd also get a lot who'd say yes."

When I first met Ron he was a practicing alcoholic. He was also married and had a baby girl. The marriage didn't last, but he has remained close to his daughter and has been a strong influence on her life. She is currently a highly sought-after Spanish commercial voice-over talent and radio and television personality in Mexico City.

I admired Ron's tremendous talent as an actor/announcer and secretly envied his great prowess with the opposite sex. Yet, I strongly disagreed with him on a number of issues, and our differences of opinion over religion, marriage and child-rearing sparked some pretty heated arguments. Nevertheless, our deep mutual love of Mexico and common professional interest in broadcasting drew us close as friends.

We also enjoyed many "happy hours" and late night parties together. One evening after several hours of heavy drinking, Ron offered to drive me home, where we could have a final nightcap or two. My family and I were then living in a subdivision called Bulevares, about 25 miles north of Mexico City. As we were driving along the freeway, Ron calmly confessed "Larry, I can't see the road."

"Well, maybe we'd better pull off." I suggested.

"That'd be fine," he answered, "except I can't tell where the exits are."

Shit! I thought, we are dead. "Well," I told Ron "just follow the guy in front of you. When he turns off, you turn too." Then I said a little prayer and promised God that I wouldn't get drunk again if He would only get us out of this.

Well, He did. The car in front of us turned off at the Bulevares exit and we found our way to my house. We celebrated our triumph with a double shot of rum and went to sleep. I kept my promise for about a week.

Ron and I made our television debut in Mexico City in 1970 on Channel 8. With two other American expatriots, Arnold Bilgore and Dale Smith, both also veteran radio broadcasters. We launched the very first live morning newscast on Mexican television. Our 7 a.m. 30-minute 5 mornings a week news program in English was called simply "The AM Report".

Ron anchored the show and reported on the world news. Arnold did sports, Dale the weather and I introed the program and covered the national and local news. Although the show lasted only nine months, due to lack of sponsors, it served as a model for Spanish language early morning news programs which followed. It was exciting to be on the cutting edge, to be pioneers. It would have been more exciting of course if we could have made a commercial success of it.

The TV station management had told us that they would handle the advertising sales for the program, but they went back on their word. Instead, they copied our format and ideas to produce a similar news program in Spanish and displaced us.

Producing the "AM Report" was both challenging and fun. Typically, we arrived at the TV station before 5 a.m. to translate, write and edit the stories which we planned to use that morning. We edited film clips, pulled slides from library files, timed and edited our scripts. It required two hours of intense preparation for a 30-minute program.

Because we were relying on non-English speaking cameramen and technical support personnel, there were numerous glitches. Ron might begin reading a story about President Nixon's trip to China and instead of rolling the appropriate film clip for that story, the technician might run one showing Mickey Mantle hitting a homerun. This would cause Ron to quip "Well, it appears that President Nixon really hit a homerun with his trip to China."

On introing the show, I was never sure if the audio engineer was going to run our signature theme and pre-recorded opening. It kept all of us on our toes. I recall one hilarious moment during the show when a prop man came running across the back of our set, tripped over a cord, flew about eight feet through the air and then landed with a loud crash just a few feet behind Ron's chair. Undaunted, and without changing his expression, Ron went right on reading the news. The rest of us could barely contain our laughter.

It was like that often. The unexpected became expected. We were working with a technical crew who had little experience. We were their mentors trying to train them to become professionals. It was often frustrating and, at times, seemed futile, but we stuck it out for almost a year.

After the show, we frequently would go to breakfast and talk shop. Then I would head for my full-time job with the American Society of Mexico. Leaving my job at the magazine around 6:30 p.m., I'd go home for supper and try to catch a couple of hours sleep before checking in at Radio Capital for my two-hour deejay show at 10:30. It made for a pretty long day.

Although short-lived, our TV program did become quite popular and it was very satisfying to receive comments from viewers both in person and by mail. Prior to doing the AM Report, I had never thought of being on television. That was something which I thank Ron for. He believed we could do it and we did.

By being involved in the program, I gained confidence in my abilities and raised my own expectations—so much so that when I decided to move back to the States I sought work in television rather than in radio. And I found it.

Larry P. Johnson

CHAPTER 31 — GOING HOME

In 1973 I decided it was time to go home, back to the United States. Mexico City was changing. When I arrived in the fall of 1957, there were less than four million residents. Now there were more than thirteen million. Pollution was a growing problem — from the dust bowl created when much of Lake Xochimilco was drained to make way for urban development, from the growing number of factories operating without emission controls, and from the hundreds of thousands of additional cars, buses and trucks spewing carbon gasses into the atmosphere.

The people were changing too. They were more materialistic, more in a hurry, more ruthlessly competitive. Mexico City was becoming a crowded, congested, hustle-bustle, dog-eat-dog rat race of a city like Chicago, New York or Los Angeles. Sentiments toward Americans or "gringos" (as we were often called) were also becoming less friendly. A tide of nationalism was sweeping the country. American companies were urged to replace their top executives with Mexican nationals.

Yes, it was time to go home. The charm and virtues of romantic Mexico, as I once saw them, were tarnishing. No doubt I was changing too. And perhaps, after 17 years, I was becoming a little homesick.

Going back to Chicago was out of the question. I wanted no part of those icy below zero winters. My body had adjusted to warmer weather, and I didn't plan to ask it to get used to frost bite and snow all over again. I wanted to pick a place which had a nice climate and where my family's bicultural background would fit right in. California seemed like a good choice. So, a trip to the golden west was in order.

My brief debut on television, doing the AM Report with Ron Fletcher a year earlier, had profoundly changed my career aspirations. It was exciting to be seen as well as heard. I decided that in moving back to the U.S., I now wanted to pursue a career in television.

Using professional broadcasting trade publications and friends to help me identify prospective job leads, I made a list of seven cities in California where there appeared to be possible opportunities for an eager, talented TV newscaster such as myself. I wrote letters and sent my resume to the program directors or station managers to set up visits and interviews. I was so naive, so unprepared, so blinded by my own conceit.

My plan was to spend two weeks visiting the 7 locations with Diana, so that she too could get a feel for each of the cities and give me her impressions of the people we met. This was going to be a major move, one we'd both have to agree on.

My friend Norman, the chef, often lived in California and I thought how neat it would be if our trip there were to coincide with him being there as well. However, I hadn't heard from Norm in a couple of years, and I didn't know how to get in touch with him. Norm and I both believed very strongly in ESP and had always done amazingly well in communicating with each other via telepathy. I decided to try projecting a message to him. It was a simple message. "Norm let me know where you are." I concentrated on that thought.

About three weeks prior to our departure, I received a call from Norm's sister Pat. She was in Mexico City on vacation. We met for dinner and I told her of Diana's and my imminent visit to California. She said that Norm was indeed in California, in Los Angeles, and gave us his address and telephone number. I called Norm the next day. He was renting a house on the outskirts of LA and said he would love to have us as house guests. Was his sister's visit and call just a coincidence?

Since this was to be primarily a business trip. We had to figure out what to do with our four children. We sent Danny to Boy Scout camp in Texas. Our two daughters, Luana and

Shirley went to Chicago to visit their aunts. Alan, who was just four, went along with us.

We spent 13 days traveling up and down the coast of California. Diana was struck at how fat many people in the States seemed and the great variety in the way they dressed. People shopped the department stores in sandals, in high heels, in slacks, in skirts, in body suits or shorts. Very democratic but quite a contrast to what we were used to in Mexico City.

The plentifulness and variety of consumer goods was dazzling and a strong attraction for both of us. At a supermarket in Mexico City, for instance, you might find three kinds of boxed cereal, while at a U.S. supermarket we found dozens to choose from. It was mind-boggling.

Diana and I liked Sacramento, the ease in getting around the city by car. It had an excellent freeway system. I was somewhat reluctance, however, to move there because of the proximity to my brother, Jim. He was a reporter for the Sacramento Bee. Jim was negative and pesimistic about my employment prospects. I worried about his depressing effect on my confidence. I decided that if I were to land a job in Sacramento I would need to remain distant from his influence. I needed to find people who would applaud me rather than criticize me, especially in the beginning. The NBC affiliate in Sacramento was looking for a Chicano person to round out their staff. I thought a good strategy would be to try to sell myself to them as a minority element. No luck.

In Fresno, I had two completely opposite reactions. The program director at one TV station was, I felt, extremely positive, impressed with my change of style from reading news to reading commercials. The manager at the other station gave us an icy cold reception.

San Diego was a big disappointment to us. Arriving by bus we were shocked and disappointed by the run-down appearance of the old terminal and the poverty we saw everywhere. Taking a taxi to the local TV station for my interview, we were told that the station manager was unavailable, called out of town unexpectedly.

Santa Barbara was a lovely city, looking from high above out across the ocean. It was so peaceful and beautiful. But my hopes of being invited to move there were dashed by the unfriendly and negative reception we received from the station manager after making us wait nearly two hours.

We agreed that San Francisco was an interesting and exciting place to visit but that we might not like to live there. The traffic was terrible and walking up and down those hills was something else. Still, I felt I made a favorable contact with the educational television station Channel 6. The program director seemed anxious to offer some positive encouragement.

Perhaps this was because he had prior experience in working with a blind person in New Jersey. In attempting to sell myself, I used the argument that a blind person might command more audience attention. He talked about the idea of doing a specialized program for the "handicapped" which could be broadened to include all minorities. It appeared to me that educational TV offered some interesting prospects by virtue of it being a younger industry. I told myself that it just might be the right time to get involved. There might be more room for opportunity, more receptivity to expressing a variety of talents in programming innovation.

I felt a good rapport with the program director in Bakersfield. He voiced admiration over my accomplishments. This gave me confidence and allowed me to speak more boldly. I hoped to buoy myself on his admiration and respect. I felt it was critical for me to win over personal support of one of these contacts in order for me to be successful in getting hired.

In all of my interviews I tried to project an air of confidence. Yet I realized that my on-camera work was limited and that I had a lot to learn. In terms of program ideas, I believed I could compete as well as the next guy. I knew it would be difficult for me to act as a critic on video presentations. As a producer or director I would have a serious handicap. I felt though that if I could ask the right questions, be aware of those aspects of video which are visual—gestures, facial expressions, body language—I might be able to compete. I resolved that I would learn as much as I could about these. I knew that it would be important to have open communication with one or more members of the TV staff in order to discuss the video aspects of the program frankly and clearly. I knew I needed to have a full understanding of what they were talking about. If I felt myself to be in a strained or constrained environment, I knew it would not work. Open and relaxed communication would be essential and would be one of the requisites to my accepting a job.

Everyone has a hidden problem or handicap. It is their weakness which can become my strength, if I can learn about it—whether they drink too much, have an inferiority complex, are overly shy, or whatever it might be—I might be able to convey my understanding and support of their problem which, in turn, might earn their understanding and support.

While visiting and talking with the people in California, I experienced a strange kind of unfamiliarity dealing with people who spoke only English. I had become so used to my environment in Mexico, so comfortable dealing with people in Spanish, people I knew and who knew me. I was accepted and had a certain reputation in Mexico which gave me prestige and position. In California, in the States, I was the stranger and everything there was strange to me.

But I was concerned about my eventual retirement, about the opportunity for my children to be exposed to their American heritage, about the sense of security of dealing with a government which was not autocratic or anti-American, about the greater availability of services for a blind person and about the general ease and convenience of living.

Yet, despite my strong commitment and diligent efforts, no job materialized for me from any of my California prospects. It took another year before I saw my goal achieved. And it wasn't to the golden west but instead to the Lone Star state, to San Antonio, where we have made our home since August, 1974.

EPILOGUE—24 YEARS AFTER

If it was my growing sense of patriotism, plus the deepening desire to give my family a chance to experience "the American dream" that caused me to leave Mexico in the summer of '74; then it was wistful nostalgia mixed with curiosity which prompted my return visit in the winter of '98.

The opportunity came suddenly and unexpectedly. Diana's niece in Mexico City called. They were having a surprise birthday party for her father, Diana's younger brother, Oscar. They wanted very much for Diana to attend. The party was planned for the following Sunday. Not much notice.

Diana acknowledged that she really wanted to go, but expressed her reservations. She was reluctant, first of all, for financial reasons, pointing out that it was a long and expensive trip to make for such a short visit. Then there was Ana, our youngest daughter, who, at 8-1/2 months pregnant, was expecting to give birth any day.

I suggested that we call the airlines to find out just how much it would cost. I learned that because Continental had just entered the market as a third carrier to provide nonstop service from San Antonio to Mexico City, the three of them, American, Mexicana and Continental had a bit of a price war going on.

237

Also, they were offering seniors an additional 10% discount. I found myself saying, "I'd like to go, too." So, without further hesitation, I made our reservations for that Friday.

The next day I called a friend of mine in the travel agency business and booked our accommodations for 3 nights at the Hotel Calinda Genova, right in the heart of the Zona Rosa. I was excited to think about what it was going to be like there, walking around in my old stomping grounds. I pondered how much things might have changed after so many years.

We were met at the airport by Diana's sister, Alma, and her son, Enrique, who drove us to our hotel. Yes, the city had grown, more freeways, more cars, and more people. The latest population estimate of 22 million made it one of the most populous cities in the world. Enrique told us that there are so many cars that authorities issue different colored license plates which limit each vehicle to be driven only three days during the week.

The Hotel Calinda Genova is, itself, an historical monument. Built just after the turn of the century, it has survived Mexico's multiple earthquakes, the Mexican revolution, and the physical and moral decline of one of Mexico City's once most fashionable tourist areas along the Paseo de La Reforma, "La Zona Rosa" or Pink Zone.

Our first shocking glimpse of this dramatic change came as we drove along Calle Florencia toward the hotel. Loudspeakers blared raucous music from a stream of bars and discos on both sides of the street, while blazing neon lights invited passersby to come and see the "hottest", most exotic, girly show in town. Enrique commented that this scene could be found now on most any street in the Zona Rosa. I felt deep sadness and disappointment. Was my entire remembered picture of Mexico to be similarly tarnished? Time would tell.

The next morning, after a satisfying continental breakfast at the hotel, consisting of fresh tropical fruit and juices, sweet rolls and coffee, we took a stroll to see what the Zona Rosa looked like by day.

The 1985 earthquake had certainly left its mark. Once familiar multi-story buildings and prosperous businesses were now gone, replaced with new ones. Other old buildings were demolished and transformed into parking lots. Everywhere were broken, uneven sidewalks, uncollected street litter, and untrimmed lawns and bushes. The Zona Rosa of today is a picture of sad neglect. Searching for the studios of XEL, Radio Capital along Insurgentes Avenue, I learned that they, together with all the other radio stations operated by Grupo ACIR had been moved, prior to the big quake, to the outskirts of Mexico City in the Lomas de Chapultepec. Later, I talked by telephone with Sr. Luis Cabero, who had been Program Director when I worked at the station and who was now Assistant Manager. He told me that Radio Capital was now an "all talk" station exclusively in Spanish. In fact, he told me that there were no longer any radio stations broadcasting in English. The cable TV industry now provided direct access to TV and radio stations in the U.S. for those who preferred listening and watching programs in English.

Weatherwise, Dame Fortune was definitely with us during our trip. The month of February in Mexico can be very erratic, windy and cold one day, hot and rainy the next. The weather during our 3-day stay was gorgeous, warm sunshine, clear blue skies, and the temperature ranging from the low 60's at night to the mid 80's during the day. No dust storms. No sign of pollution.

Several times during our visit, we were warned by friends, family members, and even local taxi drivers to be very careful when out on the street. They told us that the crime rate is frighteningly high, and American tourists are a prime target.

Despite these ominous warnings, Diana and I traveled freely, albeit somewhat prudently, to various parts of the city. We visited the church where we were married, enjoyed freshly made tortillas from a tortilla shop, strolled through a neighborhood mercado, fragrant with the smells of scores of beautiful tropical flowers and luscious fresh fruits and vegetables. We shopped for mementos and gifts at two handcraft markets and a modern, self-serve supermarket. We gladdened our palates with a wide variety of tasty and traditional Mexican dishes, some especially good because of their being home made by Diana's sister, Alma, and sister-in-law, Yolanda.

Saturday night we enjoyed dinner at La Fonda del Recuerdo restaurant on Calle Liverpool, two blocks from our hotel, with a couple we had not previously met, Ana Maria and Rogelio Parra, close friends of a friend of ours in Philadelphia. The food was wonderful, and our long conversation with this totally charming and unpretentious pair that night led to a warm and abiding friendship. Learning of my fondness for Mexican candy, "dulce de leche", (milk candy) and "cocada" (coconut candy), Ana Maria and Rogelio delivered to our hotel the next day a bag containing over 3 pounds of assorted Mexican candies. What a thoughtful gift, a real treat. Try as I might to resist, all was gone in the space of just two weeks after our return. (I did have a little help from my daughters who likewise enjoy Mexican sweets.)

The surprise birthday party for Diana's brother, Oscar, was a big success. Now retired from the Mexican telephone company, (Telefonos de Mexico), he receives a comfortable pension. He told us he spends his days drinking coffee or playing racquetball with his friends, and doting on his one-year-old grand-daughter. For him and his wife, Yolanda, it is a good life.

Diana and I returned home the following day, Monday, feeling satisfied and enriched by our visit. We were grateful — grateful to have had the chance to spend time with her family, grateful to have made new friendships and renew old ones, and grateful to have discovered that despite its problems with poverty, overpopulation and crime, Mexico still has beauty, charm, and a generous people eager to share their hospitality, their friendship, and their dreams.

ABOUT THE AUTHOR

Larry P. Johnson is totally blind, a native of Chicago, with a Bachelor's degree from the School of Speech at Northwestern University in Evanston, IL and 22 years of broadcasting experience in the U.S. and Mexico.

He made 3 trips to Mexico City as a tourist and then became a resident there for 17 years. He was one of just a few Americans licensed by the Mexican government to work in radio and television in that country. His nighttime English language program over Station XEL Radio Capital became the No.1 top radio show in Mexico City.

Larry makes his home now in San Antonio, TX. He gives motivational talks and conducts training seminars for colleges, community agencies and private corporations.

Printed in the United States
37522LVS00006B/211-309

9 781410 735904